HISTORICAL TOURS

Alexandria, Virginia

Walk the Path of America's Founding Fathers

Plan of Alexandria Town, 1749. *This 1954 souvenir map commemorates George Washington's Plan for Alexandria, created more than two centuries earlier.*

HISTORICAL TOURS

Alexandria, Virginia

Walk the Path of America's Founding Fathers

Frederick Knops

Guilford, Connecticut

To Jane, Andrew, and Stuart

Globe Pequot

An imprint of Rowman & Littlefield

Distributed by NATIONAL BOOK NETWORK

British Library Cataloguing in Publication Information Available

Library of Congress Cataloging-in-Publication Data available

ISBN (paperback) 978-1-4930-1798-0
ISBN (e-book) 978-1-4930-3049-1

♾™ The paper used in this publication meets the minimum requirements of American National Standard for Information Sciences—Permanence of Paper for Printed Library Materials, ANSI/NISO Z39.48-1992.

Contents

Map of the Land Whereon Stands the Town of Alexandria, *sketched by George Washington in 1748. Note the road leading to Hugh West's warehouse. The text on the left, inscribed by George Washington, reads "Note that on the bank fine cellars may be cut. From thence wharves may be extended on the flats without any difficulty and more houses built thereon as in Philadelphia. Good water may be got by sinking wells to small depth. The above area of 51 acres, 3 rods, 31 perch belong to Captain Philip Alexander, Mr. Hugh West. The shoals or flats about 7 feet at high water." (Library of Congress)*

Chapter I
Overview

The City of Alexandria was chartered by an act of the Colonial Virginia House of Burgesses, written in 1748 and adopted the following year. In a decision that would foreshadow the establishment of Washington D.C. as the home of the US Federal Government twenty-five years later, Alexandria was created in a location with few residents or existing structures. In fact, in 1748 no major settlement existed on the west bank of the Potomac River, save for a cluster of tobacco warehouses and a shipping pier, both owned by Hugh West, in what is now the northern end of historic Alexandria. Aside from Mr. West's small land holding, the land set aside for the new town was owned by two brothers, Philip and John Alexander, for whom the town was named.

The act required a survey of the new city and the design and naming of its streets. This survey was completed in 1749 by John West Jr., Hugh West's son, accompanied in this duty by a young George Washington, then seventeen and training in surveying. At the time, Washington divided his time between his family's plantations at Mount Vernon and Ferry Farm, the latter in Culpepper, Virginia.

This survey led to the creation and naming of the "royal streets" of Alexandria, which still comprise the heart of Old Town today. The streets oriented westward and uphill from the Potomac were named Prince, Duke, King, Cameron, Queen, Princess, and Oronoco; the latter chosen over Duchess because of the presence of the already-named Oronoco Creek in that road's path. Cameron Street was the center and focal point of the original planners' design.

This place without all question is the most pleasant and healthful place in all this country and most convenient for habitation, the air temperate in summer and not violent in winter… It aboundeth in all manner of fish. The Indians in one night commonly will catch thirty sturgeons in a place where the river is not above twelve fathoms broad. And as for deer, buffaloes, bears, turkeys, the woods do swarm with them and the soil is exceedingly fertile.

Journal of Captain Henry Fleet, entry for June 26, 1632, describing the area around the Potomac River.

Two additional streets were laid out parallel to the Potomac, running approximately north-south, named Royal and Fairfax. Water Street was also created next to the river, but only in two very short sections at the northern and southern limits of the plan.

Originally, city planners intended Cameron and Fairfax Streets to be Alexandria's primary thoroughfares, and their intersection would act as the central intersection in town. These two streets were named after Thomas, Lord Fairfax of Cameron, a Scottish peerage[1]. At the time, Lord Fairfax was one of the largest landholders in the Virginia Colony and was the only British Peer resident in North America. The intersection of these two streets came to hold the two most important buildings in the new town, Carlyle House and City Hall.

From these beginnings, as the colonies were shaped by expansion and war, so was Alexandria. Less than ten years after its founding, Alexandria rose to national prominence and became a launching point for the French and Indian War (1754-1763). Most notably, the southern flank of the war was planned at Carlyle House, in what has become known as the Congress of Alexandria. Shortly thereafter, British Gen. Edward Braddock and his army massed in Alexandria and, as they marched to war, created the road that would carry his forces west. In

[1] A peerage is any hereditary title of Great Britain

1762, at the end of that war, two streets in addition to Braddock's Road were named for men who had established themselves as friends of the American colonies during that conflict: William Pitt and Gen. James Wolfe. In addition, Gen. Richard Montgomery, who came to prominence (and earned a street in his honor) as commander of the northern flank of the Colonial forces during the Revolutionary War, fought in many of the most decisive battles of the French and Indian War.

In the years after the French and Indian War, Alexandria became a focal point in the preparation for the Revolutionary War. By that time, the settlement had become a major seaport and Mount Vernon had become George Washington's primary residence. The city saw many Virginians of national prominence visit and live here to do the work of advocating for separation from the British and preparing for war. These residents and frequent visitors would eventually provide

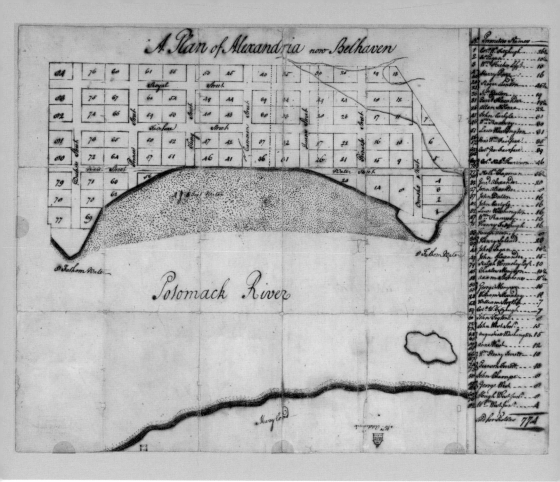

A plan of Alexandria, now Belhaven. *George Washington's original survey map, created in 1749, established the convention for Alexandria maps of positioning north toward the right. It shows only the original royal streets from Duke to Oronoco coursing away from the Potomac, plus Royal, Fairfax, and Water Streets along the river. The list on the right of the chart shows the names of those who purchased individual parcels of land during auctions held on July 13 and 14, 1749. (Library of Congress)*

a preponderance of the colonies' wartime leadership. For example, Patrick Henry, governor of Virginia and oratorical firebrand, was a frequent visitor to Mount Vernon and the city, staying at the City Hotel (now Gadsby's Tavern); Thomas Jefferson and James Madison were often seen in Alexandria as well.

After the war, other Virginians whose names now grace Alexandria's streets contributed to the formulation of the fledgling nation, including George Wythe and Edmund Pendleton, who together with Thomas Jefferson completely revised Virginia's legal code, setting a precedent for other states and the new nation. In the two decades after the end of the Revolutionary War, eighteen streets were created and named, many in honor of the generals, orators, financiers, and philosophers who helped shape the war, ensure victory, and design the new country.

The town's historic fabric and reputation grew further with the arrival of the extended Lee family, including Gen. Henry "Light Horse Harry" Lee, cavalry officer during the Revolutionary War, ninth Governor of Virginia, and father of Robert E. Lee, commander of the Confederate Forces in the American Civil War. Gen. Henry Lee settled in Alexandria in 1783, and at its peak more than forty members of the Lee family called Alexandria home, occupying about a dozen homes across the northern end of the town. The Lee family was the final one to be memorialized in the names of Old Town Alexandria streets, when shortly after Robert E. Lee's death in 1870, Water Street was renamed Lee Street, in honor of Robert and his wife Mary Anna Custis Lee.

In the late 1700s and early 1800s, Alexandria grew and added many of the buildings that define the town today, including the Lyceum, Athenaeum, City Hall, Green's Furniture Factory, and the preponderance of stately houses that remain to this day and are described in the following pages. The town's population grew slowly from its founding in 1748 to approximately seven thousand people in 1810—and stayed at that level until the Civil War, a half century later, when the population suddenly swelled to twelve thousand primarily due to the immigration of freed slaves. Canals and rail lines invaded the town in the mid-1800s, and during the Civil War the town struggled under Union occupation.

Alexandria stayed small and changed very slowly for most of its existence. Its population boom did not really begin until the second World War, when the census shows its population surpassing fifty thousand for the first time. The city largely resisted efforts at urban renewal from the 1950s to 1970s, driven by a committed band of residents that understood and cherished the history that the small town held. Residents and visitors today benefit from the slow passage of time throughout Alexandria's history, and the care that its residents take with its many treasures.

Chapter 11
Alexandria's Early Prominence: The French and Indian War

In the middle of the eighteenth century, the British colonies were bordered on all sides by French settlements—Quebec and related settlements to the north, New Orleans and related settlements to the south, and the French ownership of the lands west of the Mississippi River that would eventually comprise the Louisiana Purchase. Colonists' unease with these boundaries was aggravated by the increasing tendency for native tribes to ally with the French as a means of resisting British colonial expansion. The colonists demanded, and the British government was eager to provide, protection and opportunity for westward expansion. From the perspective of the British Crown, the American colonies offered a promising front in Britain's worldwide struggle with France for colonial domination.

In April 1755, General Braddock, Commander in Chief of the British Army in North America, convened the Congress of Alexandria in Carlyle House to plan and fund the war against New France. Attending the Congress were the governors of five of the most prominent colonies, William Shirley of Massachusetts, James Delancy of New York, Robert Hunter Morris of Pennsylvania, Horatio Sharpe of Maryland, and Robert Dinwiddie of Virginia. Historians now credit this Congress as one of the first inter-colony meetings to discuss common interests and relations with the British government.

The French and Indian War progressed on two broad fronts, north and south. In the north, in 1755, to address the French presence in what is now Maritime Canada, British colonial forces under the command of Massachusetts Governor Shirley, Sir William Johnson, and Lt. Col. William Monckton, led land campaigns in the Northeast and into Canada, supported by British General Wolfe's campaign up the Saint Lawrence River.

Simultaneously, Braddock took command of the southern flank of the war. With confidence he described his plan for the campaign to Benjamin Franklin, stating "After taking Fort DuQuesne, I am to proceed to Niagara; and having taken that, to Frontenac, if the season will allow me, as I suppose it will, for DuQuesne can hardly detain me above three or four days." In the summer of 1755, Braddock and his army departed Alexandria for the West, advancing over the plains, foothills, and mountainous terrain across Virginia, Maryland, and southern Pennsylvania, to engage the French at Fort Duquesne, near present-day Pittsburgh.

Braddock, described by historian and biographer Ron Chernow as an abusive and pigheaded commander, found it necessary to split his army into two columns, one leaving from Alexandria, and the other marshalled across the Potomac near Georgetown. The southern group had to create the road that would carry his army as he traveled. Using existing paths where available but

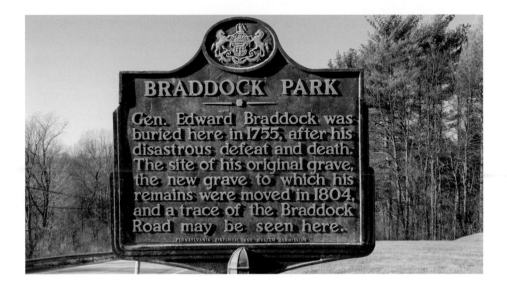

working largely through virgin territory past Cumberland, evidence of Braddock's Road can now be traced from Alexandria, through Fairfax County, and as far west as Route 40 in Pennsylvania, now known as the National Road. Braddock's intensity and relentlessness created a national asset that would become the first major transit route to the American west, carrying the settlers that drove American expansion for nearly a century. The starting point of this road can still be found off of West Street in Alexandria.

Two months after departing Alexandria, Braddock's plan came to a calamitous end. On July 9, 1755, French, Canadian, and Indian forces ambushed his troops 8 miles from Fort Duquesne, routing Braddock's army and marking the furthest point of his advance. Braddock had started with about

The historic marker indicating the location of Braddock's death and burial, off of Route 40 in western Pennsylvania

1,900 Colonial and British forces; after an arduous and laborious march across the Shenandoah mountains, more than 1,400 were lost on that day. His forces inflicted less than 100 casualties on the opposition. Among the British dead was General Braddock himself.

Assisting Braddock as aide-de-camp was Lt. Col. George Washington. Washington was instrumental in organizing the retreating army after Braddock's death and avoiding additional casualties. In 1755, Virginia Governor Dinwiddie rewarded Washington with a commission as "Colonel of the Virginia Regiment and Commander in Chief of all forces now raised in the defense of His Majesty's Colony."

The disastrous defeat served as a wake-up call to the British. British Secretary of State William Pitt decided to elevate the role of the North American conflict to the central theater of the British Crown's global conflict with France, deploying a vast array of men and armaments across the Atlantic. Historian C. P. Stacey notes in *The Dictionary of Canadian Biography*:

> On the British side particularly there was a great deployment of military power in America which for the first time was Britain's main theater of operations. In the crucial year 1759 no fewer than twenty-three British regular infantry battalions were employed in continental North America, compared with only six [against the French] in Germany.

Stacey goes on to note the full measure of the lopsided victory and enormous expense incurred by the British. In addition to these infantry, the British forces in North America also included 157 warships, 14,000 sailors of various sorts, and 2,000 pieces of artillery. Also by that year, the French American capital of Louisbourg, in the current Canadian province of Nova Scotia, had fallen to British General Wolfe, the entire French fleet in North America had been sunk or burned, and the systematic deportation and dispersion of the French settlers from what is now Canada to other British colonies, including the American colonies, was underway. In the end, it was a glorious but extremely expensive final victory over the French in North America.

The denouement of the French and Indian War, which was just one theater of the global Seven Years War between the British and the French, is difficult to separate historically from the events leading up to the American Revolutionary War. Braddock's disastrous campaign was Britain's greatest defeat in any of its colonies up to that time, and while the British were eventually triumphant against France, the war drained the crown of much of its treasury. In the years after that war, King George III sought to recoup this treasure; among the means used to restock these resources was an ever-expanding number and scale of taxes levied upon the colonies, a trend that the colonists found increasingly oppressive and led inexorably to the Revolutionary War.

Chronology of Early Alexandria

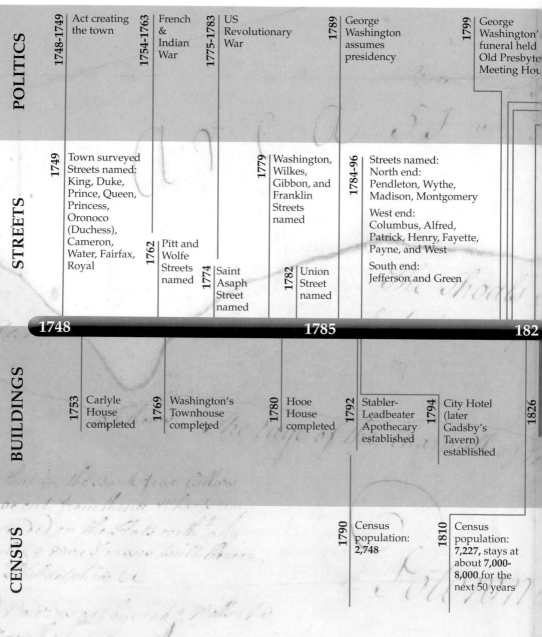

POLITICS

1748-1749	Act creating the town
1754-1763	French & Indian War
1775-1783	US Revolutionary War
1789	George Washington assumes presidency
1799	George Washington's funeral held Old Presbyte Meeting Hou

STREETS

- **1749** Town surveyed Streets named: King, Duke, Prince, Queen, Princess, Oronoco (Duchess), Cameron, Water, Fairfax, Royal
- **1762** Pitt and Wolfe Streets named
- **1774** Saint Asaph Street named
- **1779** Washington, Wilkes, Gibbon, and Franklin Streets named
- **1782** Union Street named
- **1784-96** Streets named:
  North end: Pendleton, Wythe, Madison, Montgomery
  West end: Columbus, Alfred, Patrick, Henry, Fayette, Payne, and West
  South end: Jefferson and Green

1748 — **1785** — **182**

BUILDINGS

- **1753** Carlyle House completed
- **1769** Washington's Townhouse completed
- **1780** Hooe House completed
- **1792** Stabler-Leadbeater Apothecary established
- **1794** City Hotel (later Gadsby's Tavern) established
- **1826**

CENSUS

- **1790** Census population: 2,748
- **1810** Census population: 7,227, stays at about 7,000-8,000 for the next 50 years

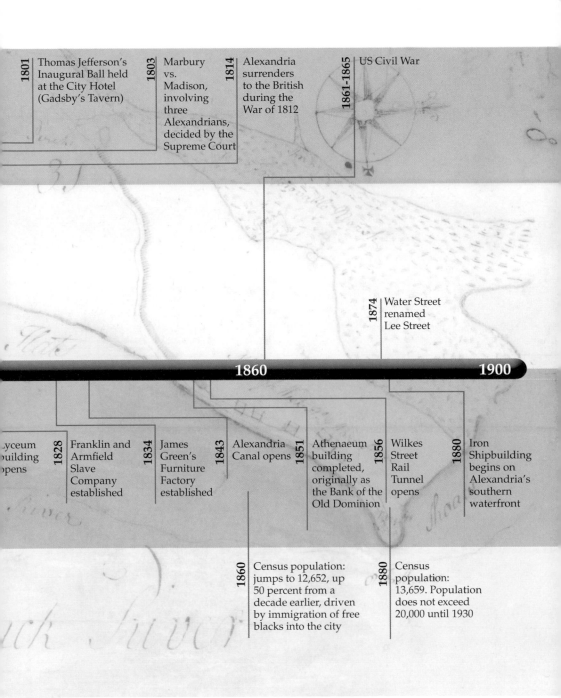

1801 Thomas Jefferson's Inaugural Ball held at the City Hotel (Gadsby's Tavern)

1803 Marbury vs. Madison, involving three Alexandrians, decided by the Supreme Court

1814 Alexandria surrenders to the British during the War of 1812

1861-1865 US Civil War

1874 Water Street renamed Lee Street

1860 | **1900**

1828 Franklin and Armfield Slave Company established

Lyceum building opens

1834 James Green's Furniture Factory established

1843 Alexandria Canal opens

1851 Athenaeum building completed, originally as the Bank of the Old Dominion

1856 Wilkes Street Rail Tunnel opens

1880 Iron Shipbuilding begins on Alexandria's southern waterfront

1860 Census population: jumps to 12,652, up 50 percent from a decade earlier, driven by immigration of free blacks into the city

1880 Census population: 13,659. Population does not exceed 20,000 until 1930

REMARKS.

ALEXANDRIA lays in Lat 38. 48. 20 North 53 2 West of the
City of Washington —
The Streets Union & Water 50 feet Washington & Franklin
& all the rest are 66 feet Wide
The Squares are 353 feet 2 In.s North & South & 246 feet 10 Inches
East & West accept the Square between Union & Water Street
which is 300 East and West of the River
The Channel at Alexandria is 1200 feet 6 to 7
fathoms at Low Water

1. W.m Fairfaxs House.
2. Camerons Mills.
3. M.r Lees House 4 Episcopal Church.
5. the Market Square 6. 7. Presbyterian & Methodist Meeting Houses.
8. 9. Scites for a Catholic & a Dutch Lutheran Church.
10. the Quakers Meeting House.

PLAN.
of the TOWN of
ALEXANDRIA,
in the District of Columbia
1748
Scale 800 to an Inch
Magnetic Variation 0. 45

GREAT HUNTING CREEK

POTOMACK RIVER

Penny Hill

Turkey Cock Alley

Church
Jefferton
Franklin
Gibson
Wilkes
Wolfe
Drake
Prince
King
Cameron
Queen
Princes
Oronoko
Pendleton
Wythe
Maddison
Montgomery

West
Pane
Fayate
Henry
Patrick
Alfred
Columb
Washin
S.t Asap
Pitt
Royal
Fairfa
Water
Union

Chapter III
Alexandria Street Names

When John West and his assistant George Washington laid out their plan for Alexandria in 1749, the city they envisioned was quite humble, including only two fully formed streets running north-south along the waterfront, and seven streets, at most three blocks in length, that ended on the bluff above the river (see map p. 4). This simple grid, which still defines Old Town Alexandria today, set the pattern for many years of expansion. John West's original streets were named after the traditional structure of royalty, with two of the streets named in honor of the city's royal patron. As the city grew from these beginnings, the subsequent street names came to reflect the country's course away from British royal rule, cataloguing the great military men, statesmen, and thinkers who won America's independence and defined the future course of the governments of Virginia and the United States. By the close of the

(on opposite page)

Plan of the Town of Alexandria in the District of Columbia, 1798. *Engraved by T. Clarke, New York. The text on the left reads "REMARKS: Alexandria lays in Lat 38.48.20 North and 2 West of the City of Washington. The Streets Union & Water 50 feet, Washington & Franklin 100, all the rest are 66 feet wide. The squares are 353 feet 2 in. North & South, & 246 feet 10 inches East & West except the square between Union & Water Street which is 300 East and West of the River. The Channel at Alexandria is 1200 & 6 to 7 fathoms at low tide. No 1 Fairfax House. 2 Cameron's Mills. 3 Mr. Lee's House. 4 Episcopal Church. 5 the Market Square. 6, 7 Presbyterian & Methodist Meeting Houses. 8, 9 Secites for a Catholic & a Dutch Lutheran Church. 10 the Quaker Meeting House." Note that in 1798 Alexandria was within the District of Columbia. (Library of Congress)*

Three Alexandrians Change the Course of US Jurisprudence
Hooe, Harper, Ramsay, and Marbury versus Madison

Brought by three Alexandrians plus the fourth eponymous plaintiff, *Marbury v. Madison* is perhaps the nation's most important Supreme Court ruling. It featured Founding Fathers on both sides, with President Thomas Jefferson and his Secretary of State James Madison pitted against the prior president, John Adams. The ruling by Chief Justice John Marshall established the concept of judicial review, instituting for all time the power of the Supreme Court to invalidate unconstitutional laws and executive actions, thereby and forever adjusting the fundamental balance of power between our three branches of government.

An example of big things having small beginnings, *Marbury* grew out of a relatively arcane dispute over government paperwork. Adams, of the Federalist Party, lost the presidential election to Jefferson on February 17, 1801. But in the weeks before Jefferson's March 4 inauguration, Adams signed into law a bill passed by the Federalist-controlled Congress that created many new judicial offices. The law took immediate effect, so Adams could fill the positions before leaving power. He did exactly that, signing the appointments for 16 new circuit judges and 42 new justices of the peace—all Federalists—just in time for the Senate to confirm them on March 3rd, Adams' last day in office. His Secretary of State John Marshall (yes, the same Marshall) rushed to deliver the signed commissions to the appointees before Jefferson's swearing-in. Political observers called these final-hour appointees Adams' "Midnight Judges."

But this being the dawn of the 19th century, courier services were not what they are today, and Marshall failed to deliver some of the signed commissions. He missed William Harper, Robert Hooe, and Dennis

Ramsay of Alexandria, as well as William Marbury of nearby Maryland. The next day, Jefferson swore his oath of office, and he immediately negated the political power play of his presidential predecessor. He and Madison, his Secretary of State, withheld the commissions intended for Harper, Hooe, Ramsay, and Marbury, denying them their appointments. The miffed would-be magistrates sued, seeking redress before the Supreme Court.

Presiding over the ensuring legal battle was Marshall, who was both Chief Justice and Adams' former Secretary of State, having held both positions simultaneously at the end of Adams' term (conflicts-of-interest policies were also not what they are today.) The case hinged on the Court's jurisdiction over *writs of mandamus*, Latin for "court orders." Ultimately the Court agreed with the plaintiffs that they were entitled to their appointments. But the Court did not order that they should receive them. Instead, Marshall ruled that a 1789 law which had expanded the Supreme Court's jurisdiction to hear cases requesting writs of mandamus, controverted the Constitution, which says that the Supreme Court may only hear such cases on appeal. In so ruling, Marshall declared that where a law contradicts the constitution, courts could— and must—strike down the law in order to preserve the primacy of our nation's charter. With this ruling, the Supreme Court's supreme authority on constitutional questions, its power of judicial review, was born.

William Marbury and his Alexandria allies never did fill their offices. Their lawsuit lost, they forfeited their fight. But the legal principle their case created lives on. *Brown v. Board of Education*, *Miranda v. Arizona*, and *Obergefell v. Hodges* are its progeny, as is nearly every landmark civil rights case in our nation's history. Marshall's *Marbury* words, which underpin all American jurisprudence, are carved onto the very walls of the Supreme Court: "It is emphatically the province of the judicial department to say what the law is."

—Contributed by John Nader, Esq

Christ Church Alexandria, *photographed looking west from the 600 block of Cameron Street, demonstrating the placement of Christ Church in Cameron Street's path. The date of the photo is disputed, cited in various sources as having been taken in various years between 1880 and 1911. The house on the right, one of the most architecturally notable in Alexandria, was built around 1800 (according to some sources as late as 1816) and was purchased in the 1820s by the Ninth Lord Fairfax, who lived there until the Civil War, when the house was possessed by Union occupiers and sold at auction in 1864. Note the cobblestone street. (Alexandria Library Special Collection)*

eighteenth century all of the streets of historic Alexandria, from Union to West, had been conceived and named.

The Royal Streets

Cameron and Fairfax: Named for Lord Thomas, Sixth Lord Fairfax, Baron of Cameron. Lord Fairfax was the primary landholder of the area between the Potomac and Rappahannock rivers in Colonial Virginia. While Fairfax's main residence was in Virginia's Northern Neck, he served on Alexandria's first Board of Trustees.

Cameron and Fairfax Streets were originally intended to be the town's two main streets. Fairfax Street was known informally as "Main Street" until the 1760s. Similarly, Cameron Street was intended as the main westerly street from the river, and initially served that purpose well as evidenced by the presence of City Hall, Carlyle House, the City Hotel (now Gadsby's Tavern), George Washington's townhouse, and many of the city's most architecturally significant homes. As originally laid out, however, Cameron Street was low and crossed the headwaters of Oronoco Creek, which made passage and maintenance difficult. In addition, in 1773, Christ Church (Anglican, later Episcopal) was built on the west side of Washington Street, directly in the path of Cameron Street. While this placement provides one of the nicest vistas in Old Town, this edifice drove most traffic and commerce 1 block south to King

From Fredericksburg to Alexandria we found frightfully bad roads. The latter place is situated on the river. Its streets are laid out after the plan of Philadelphia and upon a large scale, in anticipation of a great city. Considering its peculiar advantages of position at the head of the bold navigation of one of the noblest rivers in the world, I see nothing to prevent the anticipation [from] being fully realized.

Memoirs of Elkanah Watson including Journals of Travels in Europe and America from 1772-1842. Ed. Winslow Watson. 1968 edition.

The Strand between Duke and Prince Streets, *photographed in 1865. The small building on the far left no longer exists, replaced by the Strand shops and parking. The twin buildings in the middle of the Strand remain, although altered; the slightly farther one houses Chadwick's restaurant. The two-story building at the far end of the strand is now one story and contains Big Wheel Bikes. Where the ships and piers are shown in the foreground is now reclaimed land providing the parking lot for the Dandy; farther back Founders Park now sits on reclaimed land as well. The photo was taken from the top of the Pioneer Mill, which at six stories was the highest structure in Alexandria at the time. (Library of Congress)*

Street, which to this day serves as the primary commercial thoroughfare of the historic district.

Duke, Prince, King, Queen, Princess, and Oronoco: Originally named after the common royal hierarchy. Any consideration of maintaining symmetry by naming the street north of Princess as "Duchess" was quickly abandoned due to the practical matter that this street passed near the spring that served as the headwater of the small Oronoco Creek. This stream, and consequently the street, were named for the Oronoco variety of tobacco, which was commonly grown in Virginia. At the time of the city's founding, the original rolling road, in which hogsheads (barrels) of tobacco were rolled to Hugh West's warehouse, passed nearby.

The names of these streets have not always been assured: a century later, in 1855, the *Alexandria Gazette* reported:

> *George Washington Parke Custis, Martha Washington's grandson, recommended to Alexandrians in a speech delivered on General Washington's birthday, February 22, 1855, that the 'Citizens of the town abolish royalty from their streets, and in place of King, Prince, Duke, etc., etc., to call them Marshall, Monroe, Mercer, and other names distinguished in our revolutionary annals.'*

Alexandria Academy, *at the corner of Wolf and Washington Streets. An inscription on the site reads "On 17 Dec. 1785, George Washington endowed a school here in the recently established Alexandria Academy 'for the purpose of educating orphan children.' In 1812, an association of free African Americans founded its own school here in space vacated by white students. Young Robert E. Lee attended another school in the Academy from 1818 to 1823, when it closed and the building was sold. During the Civil War the Academy served as a freedman's hospital. Returned to the Alexandria School Board in 1884, the Alexandria Academy was used as a school and administrative facility until 1982. The Historic Alexandria Foundation restored it in 1999." (Alexandria Library Special Collection)*

There is no evidence that this recommendation was considered by city leadership.

The Streets of War

In the years following establishment of Alexandria's royal streets in 1749, the town quickly took shape on the bluff above the Potomac. So quick was its growth, in fact, that the ever-increasing population and industry required the creation of twenty additional streets by the end of the century. The names of these streets mirror the early years of the country: shaped largely by war and the ongoing debate among the founding fathers as to the shape and trajectory of the new system of government.

Streets Commemorating
the French and Indian War

Braddock: Named for General Edward Braddock (1695-1755). Braddock, born in Scotland, entered the British military in the Scottish Coldstream Guards at age fifteen. He first saw battle in 1747, at age fifty-two, in Holland. In 1755 Braddock was appointed as Commander in Chief of the British forces in all thirteen colonies. Landing in Virginia in February 1755, he immediately set upon the planning of the North American campaign against the French *(see also page 7)*.

Pitt: Named for William Pitt (1708-1778). First Earl of Chatham and Member of Parliament, Pitt was one of the most significant supporters and financiers of the British North American colonies. Pitt also served as Britain's Secretary of State during the Seven Years War (1756-1763) against France that was fought across Europe, as well as across their North American and African colonies. In 1758, after initial setbacks in the North American – where these skirmishes now referred to now as the French and Indian War – Pitt put into place a strategy for focusing his resources and firepower against France in the German theater and simultaneously leveraging Britain's tremendous naval superiority to engage and capture French forces around the globe, primarily in North America. As a result of the success of this strategy, Pitt is often credited as one of the primary forces behind Britain's rise to dominance in world affairs in the late 1700s.

City Hall Market,
photographed around 1915. At the time this photo was taken, the City Hall building was u-shaped, with the central portion and main entrance facing Cameron Street, and with short wings along Fairfax and Royal Streets (see the map on page 77). The photograph is taken facing west, from inside the courtyard formed by the shape of the building, a position approximately where the market square bandstand is today. The buildings on the left side of the photo no longer exist. (Alexandria Library Special Collection)

Wolfe: Named for Gen. James Wolfe (1727-1759). Wolfe was considered the greatest hero of the French and Indian War in the Colonies and in Britain. During the Seven Years War, Wolfe was initially posted in a defensive position in Canterbury, England, and then sent to engage the French in Rochefort, France. In 1758, Wolfe was promoted to Brigadier General and assigned to lead the British forces in their engagement of the French in Cape Breton Island, Nova Scotia, at the mouth of the Saint Lawrence River. Wolfe's army and navy traveled up the Saint Lawrence through a number of skirmishes and laid siege to Quebec in the spring of 1759, against French General Montcalm. This siege culminated on September 13, in the Battle of the Plains of Abraham outside the Quebec fortress. The British were victorious in this battle, but both generals, Wolfe and Montcalm, died from wounds sustained there.

Streets Commemorating the Revolutionary War and the Founding Fathers

Fayette: Named for the Marquis de Lafayette (1757-1834), French nobleman. During the American Revolution, Lafayette served as a major general in the Continental Army under Gen. George Washington. While commanding the Colonial forces, Washington relied most heavily on two of his aides and confidants, Lafayette and Alexander Hamilton, neither of whom were native to the American colonies. During the war, Lafayette traveled to France to negotiate financial support for the revolution.

After the war, in 1784, he returned to America and included visits to Alexandria and Richmond, where he addressed the House of Delegates and called for "liberty of all mankind," including the emancipation of slaves in the United States. Lafayette visited the United States again in 1824-1825 to celebrate the nation's fiftieth anniversary. During his tour, he twice visited Alexandria. On the first occasion, in October 1824, his arrival was celebrated with a parade and celebration at Gadsby's Tavern, attended by Secretary of State John Quincy Adams one year before his election to the presidency. Lafayette's last visit to Alexandria occurred on February 21, 1825, on the centennial anniversary of George Washington's birth.

[The Potomac…] is the sweetest and greatest river I have ever seene, so that the Thames is but a little finger to it. There are noe marshes or swampes about it, but solid firme ground, with great variety of woode, not choaked up with undershrubs, but commonly so farre distant from each other as a coach and fower horses may travel without molestation.

Father Andrew White, Jesuit missionary, 1634, from A Briefe Relation of the Voyage unto Maryland

Franklin: Named for Benjamin Franklin (1706-1790), American statesman, author, inventor, printer, scientist, and contributor to the Declaration of Independence. Franklin was one of America's greatest diplomats, spending most of 1764 to 1775 in England, writing, speaking, and working prodigiously on behalf of the colonies. After a brief return to the colonies spent representing Pennsylvania at the Continental Congress, he returned to Europe and served as Ambassador to France from 1776 to 1785. He was also granted a special commission from Congress in 1777 to serve as minister to Spain. In his later years, Franklin wrote portions of his autobiography while in residence with the Bishop of Saint Asaph.

Earlier, in 1755, Franklin played an interesting role in Edward Braddock's campaign. Franklin, in his autobiography, tells of meeting with Braddock several times, advising him on the provisioning of his army in preparation for the western campaign. At one point, Franklin traversed the region from Philadelphia to Lancaster, equipped by Braddock with 800 British pounds sterling, to acquire for the campaign "one hundred and fifty wagons, with four horses and a driver each, and fifteen hundred pack horses." Franklin added two hundred pounds of his own money to support the acquisition of supplies and petitioned the Pennsylvania Assembly successfully for additional funds.

Although residential in nature, Franklin Street was laid out to be 100 feet wide, equal to the width of Washington Street and double the width of most Alexandria streets, to accomodate the increased traffic related to the new but rapidly growing shipyard stretching from Wolfe to Franklin Streets (*see page 96*).

Green: Named for Gen. Nathanael Greene (1742-1786); note the misspelling. General Greene is considered one of the great strategists of the Revolution. At the start of the war, Greene, an ex-Quaker and ironmonger from Rhode Island, commanded the Rhode Island Militia, serving with distinction at the battles of Brandywine and Trenton. George Washington later appointed Greene Commander of the Revolutionary Army in the South. In this role, he drove the British out of the Carolinas and Virginia. General Greene visited Alexandria in September 1783, staying at Mount Vernon; he took ill during the visit and he resided with friends in the town for six days.

Henry: Named for Patrick Henry (1736-1799). Henry was one of the most passionately outspoken patriots during the Revolutionary period, famous for his speech that included the line, "Give me liberty or give me death." In 1774, he, George Mason, and George Washington met at Mount Vernon to discuss the increasing tensions between the colonies and the British crown. The statement they drafted, known as the Fairfax Resolves, laid out the American concerns regarding British rule, governance, and taxation; called for a congress of the colonies; and became a template for the Declaration of Independence written two years later. In 1776, Henry was elected governor of Virginia, and was re-elected for three terms. After being succeeded by Thomas Jefferson, he was again elected to the office in 1784. Henry was so highly revered that Alexandrians named two streets for him, Patrick and Henry.

Jefferson: Named for Thomas Jefferson (1743-1826), third president of the United States, primary author of the Declaration of Independence, architect, and diplomat. Jefferson began his political career as a lawyer and as a member of the Colonial Virginia House of Burgesses, representing Albemarle County from 1769 to 1775. In 1775, he was selected to represent Virginia at the Second Continental Congress. Although a notable thinker and statesman, he was better known for his writing than speaking abilities. Referred to as the "silent member" of the Continental Congress, Jefferson nevertheless wrote or revised the majority of the Declaration of Independence. In 1776, he returned to Virginia to serve in the new Virginia Assembly, and three years later, at the age of thirty-six, was elected governor of Virginia.

The new American Congress asked Jefferson to succeed Benjamin Franklin as Minister to France in 1785; George Washington recalled Jefferson with an invitation to serve as his Secretary of State in 1790. While serving in that role Jefferson made his first recorded visit to Alexandria and Mount Vernon, with at least six additional visits recorded in subsequent years. Due to philosophical differences regarding the powers of the executive branch and practical disagreements with Washington over the United States' relationship and Britain and France, Jefferson resigned from Washington's cabinet in 1793 and returned to Monticello. Washington, it is said, never forgave Jefferson for this betrayal.

After serving as James Madison's vice president (1796-1800), Jefferson was elected to the presidency in 1800. Reporting on his inauguration, the *Alexandria Times* noted with pride that a detachment of the Alexandria militia accompanied Jefferson on his walk from his hotel to the ceremony at the capital, and also reported that the Alexandria militia fired the honorary salute at several points during the ceremonies.

In spite of Jefferson's estrangement from George Washington, one last recorded visit to Alexandria and Mount Vernon occurred in 1801, two years after Washington's death.

Madison: Named for James Madison (1751-1836), fourth president of the United States and the primary author of the US Constitution and Bill of Rights. In 1780, Madison was chosen to represent Virginia in the Continental Congress (1780-1783 and 1786-1788). Although its youngest delegate, he played a major role in the deliberations of that body, taking the floor to speak more than 150 times. Madison co-wrote The Federalist Papers along with Alexander Hamilton and John Jay, who, like him, advocated strongly for state assemblies to adopt the constitution. Madison served briefly in the Virginia House of Delegates from 1784 to 1786, and then served in the US House of Representatives from 1789 to 1797, writing the Bill of Rights and advocating for its adoption by that body. Madison served as President Thomas Jefferson's secretary of state, and in 1809 succeeded him to the presidency. His administration was most notable for its involvement in the War of 1812, which conclusively ended British designs on North America.

James Madison was a frequent visitor at Mount Vernon and stayed at Gadsby's Tavern on numerous occasions, and on one occasion stayed at Mount Vernon while Washington was absent: On February 16, 1789, Washington wrote to Madison, congratulating him on his election to Congress, and inviting him to stay at Mount Vernon during his travel to New York. Madison arrived in Mount Vernon approximately one week later. Due to a severe winter storm, Madison was forced to reside at Mount Vernon until March 2nd without seeing his friend Washington, who was delayed in Baltimore by the same storm during that entire time.

Montgomery: Named for Richard Montgomery (1738-1775). Montgomery fought in several battles in the northern campaigns of the French and Indian War, including the Siege of Louisbourg, Battle of Ticonderoga, Capture of Fort Carillon, and the decisive capture of Montreal. After the French and Indian War, he returned to his home in Ireland, but resettled in New York in 1774. At the outbreak of the Revolutionary War, Montgomery was appointed brigadier general under George Washington. In June 1775, Washington asked Generals Schuyler and Montgomery to lead a campaign against the British forces in northern New York and Canada to secure the Saint Lawrence River as an important resupply route for the Colonial forces. During the campaign, General Schuyler's health failed and Montgomery assumed sole leadership of the campaign. The campaign accumulated victories at Fort Ticonderoga, Saint Johns, and Montreal; however, during the siege of Quebec, General Montgomery was killed and the Colonial forces retreated.

A century after the Revolution, the *Alexandria Gazette* reported on January 1, 1876, that among the reminiscences of the townsfolk was that in 1776:

> . . . *all were waiting with anxiety to hear the news from Canada, where it was known that Montgomery and Arnold were moving to the contest of Quebec. None knew then that on the night before, the assault of Quebec had been made in vain and that the Continental troops had been driven back with Arnold wounded and Montgomery slain. Years*

At Alexandria the Potomac rolls its majestic stream with sublimity and grandeur, sixty gunships may lie before the town, which stands upon its lofty banks, commanding, to a great extent, the flatter shore of Maryland. This town is rapidly on the increase, and . . . cannot fail of becoming one of the first cities of the new world.

The Marquis de Chastellux.
Travels in North America,
volume III, 1780-1782.

afterwards our people gave Montgomery a monument by giving his name to a street.

Patrick: *See Henry (page 27)*

Payne: Named for William Payne, resident of Alexandria. While little is known about Payne, the historical record shows him as a colonel in the Revolutionary War, surveyor of Fairfax County, and one of the original trustees of the town. He was also a friend of George Washington and served as pallbearer at his funeral in 1799.

Pendleton: Named for Edmund Pendleton (1721-1803). Pendleton was president of the Virginia Convention of 1776, which adopted his resolution instructing Virginia delegates to the Continental Congress to propose independence from Great Britain. After the declaration, he became the first speaker of Virginia's new House of Delegates. Pendleton, along with Thomas Jefferson and George Wythe, revised and rewrote Virginia's legal code from 1776 to 1779. When Virginia created a Supreme Court of Appeals in 1778, Pendleton was appointed its first president and served until his death. In 1788, he was unanimously appointed president of the Virginia Ratifying Convention. Thomas Jefferson said of Pendleton: "Taken in all he was the ablest man in debate I ever met."

The 200 Block of South Saint Asaph Street, *looking north, photographed during the Civil War. This photo is occasionally mislabeled as South Lee Street due to the resemblance of the Greek Revival building in the distance to the Athaneum. This building was constructed in 1840 as the Second Presbyterian Church, an offshoot of the congregation at the Old Presbyterian Meeting House. After the Civil War, the building housed the Veteran's Reserve Headquarters. The building has been renovated and expanded several times since this photo, including a restyling from Greek Revival to Romanesque in 1889. Most recently this building has housed an architectural center. The white building in the middle of the photo no longer stands; it was removed to accommodate the US District Court building on the 200 block of South Washington and a parking lot behind it. The two brick residences in the foreground remain, although somewhat modified. The building at 209 South Saint Asaph was used as the residence and headquarters of the Military Governor of Virginia, Gen. John Slough. (Alexandria Library Special Collection).*

Washington: Named for George Washington (1732-1799); resident of Alexandria, commander of the Virginia Regiment during the French and Indian War, Commander in Chief of the Continental Army during the Revolutionary War, and first President of the United States. After commanding the colonial forces to victory, Washington attended the Constitutional Convention in Philadelphia in 1787, and was unanimously elected president of the convention. After serving as president for eight years (1789-1797), Washington retired from public life. Washington's primary residence during his adult life was at Mount Vernon, approximately 10 miles south of Alexandria, and the town of Alexandria served as the primary location for his commercial affairs. He maintained a townhouse in Alexandria, at 508 Cameron Street (between Pitt and Saint Asaph streets), and had a designated pew at Christ Church, 2 blocks away.

Wythe: Named for George Wythe (1726-1806). Wythe is regarded as one of the greatest legal minds in American history. In the three years following 1776, along with Edmund Pendleton and Thomas Jefferson, Wythe completely revised and restructured the Virginia state code of law. In 1779, Jefferson and other officials of the College of William and Mary in Williamsburg, Virginia, created the first Chair of Law in an American institution of higher learning and appointed Wythe as the first professor to receive that honor. In that position, he educated America's earliest college-trained lawyers, among them John Marshall, future Chief Justice of the US Supreme Court, and James Monroe, future US president. Wythe was also a signer of the Declaration of Independence.

Streets Commemorating the Civil War

Lee: Named for both Robert E. Lee (1807-1870) and Mary Anna Custis Lee (1808-1873). Robert E. Lee was Commanding General of the Confederate Armies during the American Civil War. The Lee family held a residence on Oronoco Street in Alexandria, and Lee resided here often during his early life. Originally named Water Street, it was renamed (variously in 1870, 1873, or 1874, depending on the source), after General Lee's death. Lee's wife, Mary Anna Custis Lee, was the daughter of George Washington Parke Custis, George Washington's step-grandson and adopted son.

Streets Commemorating Other Historical Figures

Alfred: Named for King Alfred the Great (848-899), king of the Anglo-Saxons and father of British Common Law. Alfred is often considered one of the greatest British monarchs due to his unification of various Anglo-Saxon tribes in the British Isles and his consolidation of written and unwritten laws into the first single written code of law.

Historian Barbara Yorke states that during the latter half of the eighteenth century, there

The statue Appomattox, *at the intersection of South Washington and Prince Streets, erected in 1899 to memorialize Alexandria's Confederate soldiers. This photo was taken around 1920. (Library of Congress)*

was a resurgence on both sides of the Atlantic in the study of Alfred's reign and code, including the republication of Alfred's code, in 1773, in a single volume widely available in Britain and the American Colonies. Study of King Alfred's reign greatly influenced Thomas Jefferson and shaped the work of Wythe and Pendleton. Early in their relationship, Wythe encouraged Jefferson to seek out and learn from historic books of law, with a particular focus on the Anglo-Saxon basis of English common law. Jefferson came to admire Alfred and proposed that the work of constructing a new country be based on Alfred's precedent. In a letter to Pendleton, Jefferson wrote

"Has not every restitution of the antient Saxon laws had happy effects? Is it not better now that we return at once into that happy system of our ancestors, the wisest and most perfect ever yet devised by the wit of man?"

Jefferson also noted that Alfred's codification of the law drew upon the laws of the home countries of the early settlers of the British Isles, including early French and Dutch laws and traditions, but that Alfred was careful to avoid implying any form of allegiance to or control by the countries from which the settlers had emigrated—a useful point in the argument for Colonial independence.

Columbus: Named for Christopher Columbus (1451-1506), discoverer of the New World. During his four voyages across the Atlantic spanning 1492 to 1503, Columbus never made land north of the Bahamas and Cuba, and thus likely never saw the mainland of North America. The Chesapeake Bay was to remain undiscovered by Europeans until Spanish explorer Lucas Vasquez sent a northward expedition from his base of operations on the island of Hispaniola; the Potomac River was likely first sited by Captain John Smith during his explorations of the Chesapeake Bay in 1607.

While Christopher Columbus has no direct link to the geography that was to become Alexandria or Virginia, an interesting story is told about Thomas Jefferson's admiration for Columbus: When Jefferson was Ambassador to the Court of France in 1784, he saw a painting of Columbus, admired it, and ordered a copy made for himself. It was sent back to his home in Monticello and hung there for many years. It now hangs in Boston at the Massachusetts Historical Society.

Gibbon: Named for Edward Gibbon (1737-1794), author of *The History of the Decline and Fall of the Roman Empire*, published in 1776. This text gained wide distribution across the American colonies and helped shape Colonial leaders' thinking about the causes of the British Empire's decline, and, by comparison, the philosophical outlines of the new American national government. Both George Washington and Thomas Jefferson were known to have owned and studied copies of this book.

Saint Asaph: Named for Dr. Jonathan Shipley (1714-1788), Bishop of St. Asaph Cathedral in Wales from 1769 until his death. Shipley was an outspoken supporter of the colonies, their cause, and their independence, throughout his public life. He rose to prominence when he was chosen to give the sermon culminating the 1773 annual meeting to the British Society for the Propagation of the Gospel. His speech focused on the British government's ill treatment of the American colonies. The society reprinted the sermon and distributed it widely. Benjamin Franklin, a close friend, published and distributed the sermon in the American colonies. In a speech before the British Parliament's House of Lords, the bishop stated: "My Lords, I look upon North America as the only great nursery of freedom now left upon the face of the earth."

Union: Created by the landfill and erosion from the high ground of Fairfax and Water Streets. It was named shortly after the Revolutionary War (not the Civil War, as often thought), in honor of the union of the colonies into one country.

West: Named for the West family, including Hugh West (1705-1754), the owner of dock, warehouse, and tobacco inspection station on the Potomac River, known as West's Point, that was to become the town of Alexandria; Hugh's son, John West Jr. (c. 1727-1776) who was appointed by the Virginia House of Burgesses to be the surveyor of the town alongside George Washington; and Hugh's daughter Sybil, who became the wife of John Carlyle, builder of the Carlyle House. More generally, the West family was one of the most influential in the area during Colonial times, with significant land holdings dating back to Thomas West, Second Baron De La Warr

(1556-1602). The Delaware Bay, and later the State of Delaware, were named after the Baron De La Warr.

Baron Thomas West and his son, John West (1590-1659), secured 600 acres of land on the York River, followed by other grants and acquisitions between the York and Potomac Rivers eventually totaling more than 3,000 acres. Jim Bish, in his extensive chronicle of the West family, describes how, several generations later, in the 1730's, descendent Hugh West purchased 30 acres on the Potomac River near its northern limit of navigability. He quickly established the pier and warehouse to support the export of tobacco, and sought and was granted a license from the Virginia House of Burgesses as an Inspector of Tobacco. In 1740, he added a ferry service, also licensed by the House of Burgesses, to the Maryland shore. The tobacco inspection and storage business was a near-monopoly in the area; the closest similar facility in Virginia was 30 miles to the south, also on the Potomac. Due to his business success and his lineage, West was very familiar with both the Washington and Fairfax families, and had much to gain from the establishment of a town around the location of his business. Hugh's son John West Jr. played an integral role as the surveyor of the town. In later years John West Jr. served under George Washington in the 1754 exploration of French positions near the Monongahela and Ohio Rivers that led to the establishment of Fort Necessity and served as a pre-cursor to the French and Indian War; served as one of the first Trustees of Alexandria alongside George Washington, Thomas Fairfax, John Carlyle, and William Ramsay; and served as a representative to the 1776 Constitutional Convention.

Wilkes: Named for John Wilkes (1727-1797), English statesman and journalist who was an early advocate of the freedom of the press, campaigner against British political corruption, and champion of the cause of American independence. In 1771, Wilkes was instrumental in pressuring the British Parliament to concede the right of printers to publish verbatim accounts of parliamentary debates. In 1776, he introduced the first bill for parliamentary reform in the British Parliament. Wilkes' fight against British parliamentary corruption is reflected in US constitutional principles of freedom of the press and provisions that require Congress to seat any member elected legally.

The Master Map

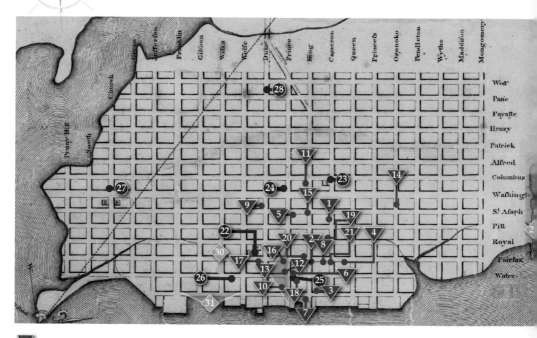

▼ RESIDENCES and BUSINESSES

1. **George Washington Townhouse**: 508 Cameron Street
2. **Ramsay House**: 211 King Street
3. **Ramsay Warehouse**: 101 King Street
4. **Dalton House**: 207 North Fairfax Street
5. **Brown House**: 517 Prince Street
6. **William Fairfax House**: 207 Prince Street
7. **John Fitzgerald Warehouse**: 100 South Union Street
8. **Carlyle House**: 121 North Fairfax Street
9. **Lawrason House**: 301 South Saint Asaph
10. **Shreve & Lawrason Warehouse**: 100 Prince Street
11. **Fowle House**: 711 Prince Street
12. **Hooe House**: 201 South Lee Street
13a. **Captains Row**: 100 Block of Prince Street
13b. **Gentry Row**: 200 Blocks of Prince Street
14. **The Robert E. Lee Boyhood Home**: 607 Oronoco
15. **Site of the Marshall House Hotel**: Corner of King and Pitt Streets
16. **James Green's Furniture Factory**: 200 South Fairfax Street
17. **Friedson's Grocery Store**: 300 South Fairfax
18. **Mutual Ice Company Distribution Building**: 110 South Lee Street
19. **Gadsby's Tavern**: 134 North Royal Street
20. **Stabler-Leadbeater Apothecary**: 105 & 107 South Fairfax Street
21. **Bank of Alexandria**: 133 North Fairfax Street

● RELIGIOUS and CULTURAL INSTITUTIONS

22. **Old Presbyterian Meeting House**: 321 South Fairfax Street
23. **Christ Church Alexandria**: 114 North Washington Street
24. **The Lyceum**: 201 South Washington Street
25. **Athenaeum**: 201 Prince Street
26. **Free Methodist Church**: 424 South Lee Street
27. **Alexandria Contraband and Freedman's Cemetery**: 1001 South Washington Street
28. **Franklin and Armfield Slave Company, now the Freedom Museum**: 1315 Duke Street

◆ INFRASTRUCTURE

29. **Alexandria Canal**: Canal Center Plaza, Montgomery Street at the Potomac River
30. **Wilkes Street Tunnel**: 200 block of Wilkes Street
31. **Hunter Shipyard**: 400-600 Union Street

Chapter IV
Residences and Businesses

George Washington Townhouse: 508 Cameron Street

As Alexandria was established and George Washington increasingly used the young town as a basis for trade, it would have been natural for him to establish a residence for extended stays in town. It would have been just as natural for him to choose Cameron Street—the main street and most prestigious address—for that residence. George Washington's Townhouse, although now a modern reconstruction, is one of a few present examples of the rectangular wood-clad residences that were the most familiar form of architecture in the earliest days of the village. Washington's Townhouse, along with the very similar Ramsay and Dalton Houses, and the unique J. D. Brown House, are the best examples of architecture dating from the very first years of the village.

George Washington's original purchase of land in May 1763 gave him ownership of a much larger lot, of about one quarter of the block, that encompassed the current plot that holds the house. The residence was completed in 1769. Thereafter the property often welcomed George Washington and members of his immediate family, and was often used for extended family and friends as well. Philip Marsteller, who served as one of President Washington's pallbearers, lived in this house in 1797, two years before Washington's death. The Washingtons also lent the house to Fanny Bassett Washington, Martha Washington's niece, who resided there from 1794 to 1795.

The original house was torn down in 1855; in 1960, Governor of Virginia Richard Lowe purchased the property and reconstructed the house. Today it serves as a private residence.

Ramsay House: 211 King Street
Ramsay Warehouse: 101 King Street

The Ramsay House was the primary residence of father William Ramsay (?-1785) and son Dennis Ramsay (1756-1810), both prominent figures in the early years of Alexandria. William Ramsay was among a group of Scottish settlers, including John Carlyle *(see page 55)*, who searched the upper reaches of the navigable Potomac for a site for a new shipping port. Ramsay and Carlyle selected Alexandria's location and were the successful petitioners to the Virginia House of Burgesses to have the land ceded from Fairfax County to form the new city. Like Carlyle, Ramsay was one of the first city trustees, and purchased land in the first auction in 1749. Purchased at this time were the lot at 211 King Street on which he placed his home, and a waterfront lot at 101 King Street that he used for his business.

Not all of the Ramsay House is original to this location. Unique among the earliest buildings of Old Town, the Ramsay House was started by transporting a small building by barge from elsewhere on the Potomac— there are no records of where or when the journey began—to the foot of King Street and then hauling it up that street to be placed on the building site. The rest of the house was later built around this humble beginning.

While it is safe to think that William Ramsay would have placed a pier and some sort of storage facility on the lot at 101 King Street, there is no record of a structure until

The Ramsay House *photographed before being consumed by fire in 1942 and restored by the City of Alexandria. At that time it held a shop of cigars, cigarettes, and loose tobacco. The shopkeeper lived in the residence above. (Alexandria Library Special Collection)*

1803, when a three-story brick building likely built by William's son Dennis appears on a survey completed by a local insurance society. In the years before 1803, the Ramsays, like many other owners of waterfront lots on the land at the top of the bluff, would have taken soil from above the bluff and filled in the marshy land below so that their wharf could provide access farther into the Potomac.

William Ramsay's son Dennis inherited the house and business upon William's death in 1785. Dennis continued his father's trade of exporting primarily tobacco and importing general wares for the town. When the Revolutionary War interrupted the proceedings of both the town and the Ramsay family, Dennis served as an officer in the Continental Army. He went on to serve in various political posts in Alexandria, culminating in his election as mayor in 1789. During his term, he gave a farewell address in front of Wise's Tavern at the corner of Fairfax and Cameron Streets to celebrate Washington's departure to New York to serve as the country's first president. Both William and Dennis Ramsay were close to George Washington and his family; Dennis Ramsay served as a pallbearer at Washington's funeral.

Dennis Ramsay was also one of four plaintiffs (along with William Harper, Robert Hooe, and William Marbury) in Marbury vs. Madison (1803), widely viewed as one of the most significant cases heard and decided by the US Supreme Court.

The building continued to be the residence of the Ramsays for more than a century, after which it was used by subsequent owners for a variety of businesses, including a tavern and grocery store. After being damaged by fire in 1942, it was purchased by the city in 1956, restored, and is now used as the Alexandria Visitors' Center.

Dalton House: 207 North Fairfax Street

The Dalton House, along with George Washington's Townhouse, the J.D. Brown House, and the Ramsay House, comprise three of the earliest buildings of Old Town

The Dalton House, *photographed around 1925 (Alexandria Library Special Collection)*

Alexandria and have similar architectural styles. The brick façade and single dormer window of the current Dalton House are a modern addition; the sides and rear of the house are true to the original appearance.

The Dalton House was built around 1777 by John Dalton, an importer of sugar, rum, and other general merchandise as well as slaves, and exporter of tobacco, wheat, and other products made in Virginia. Dalton was George Washington's friend and served as Washington's agent for the products grown and manufactured at Mount Vernon.

Dalton served on the vestry of Christ Church (*see page 81*) and as a trustee of the town of Alexandria. He also worked in partnership with John Carlyle (*see page 55*) for more than twenty-five years. The Carlyle-Dalton Landing, including a pier and small warehouse, was located at the corner of Cameron and Water (now Lee) Streets.

J.D. Brown House: 517 Prince Street

The John Douglass Brown House is possibly the oldest standing structure in Old Town Alexandria, and one of the least modified of all houses dating from this era. There is evidence that this building incorporated elements of a prior structure dating to around 1734. The original building—the section facing the street—is of similar style and construction as the Ramsay, Washington, and Dalton Houses.

The rear of the J. D. Brown House, *photographed in 1936 (Alexandria Library Special Collection)*

The land for this home was purchased in December 1774 by Patrick Murray, who built the main structure on the lot during the subsequent year. The house and land were then purchased in 1816 by John Douglass Brown and remained in the same family until the late twentieth century.

The building was expanded to the north at least twice between 1774 and 1800. When viewed from the west (uphill) side, the red-hued wooden siding shows the original construction of the home. The original siding and the nails used to secure the siding to the timber framing were discovered during a renovation in 2000. The stone foundation, visible from the street, is also original to the house.

William Fairfax House: 207 Prince Street

The William Fairfax House, on what is now known as Gentry Row, was built by Col. William Fairfax in 1753 after his arrival as the local agent of his uncle, the Sixth Lord Cameron of Fairfax. Prior to that appointment, William was a wanderer, albeit a well-connected one, who left his family estate as a young man to serve as a customs agent in Barbados, followed by a stint as Chief Justice of the Bahamas. When the Sixth Lord Fairfax learned in 1732 of the death of the agent for his holdings in the Virginia colony, which exceeded 5 million acres bounded by the Potomac and Rappahannock Rivers, he asked William to serve as the replacement and secured for him the position of the colony's customs agent.

By then in his early forties, William Fairfax originally set up his household in Belvoir Manor, a property neighboring George Washington's Mount Vernon. A decade later William Fairfax bought the Prince Street lot during Alexandria's first land auction, and established the home on Prince Street much as George Washington established his townhouse on Cameron Street. William and his son George Fairfax were both members of the House of Burgesses of the colony of Virginia, and both served as Trustees of Alexandria upon its founding. William Fairfax sold the property in 1771 and returned to England with his family.

The house and lot were purchased by Robert Adam in 1771 and then by Captain

The William Fairfax House *at 207 Prince Street, photographed in 1936 (Alexandria Library Special Collection)*

John Harper in 1773. The current structure on the property dates to this era. Captain Harper owned numerous other houses on the 100 and 200 blocks of Prince Street. Captain Harper's role as the primary developer of the 100 block of Prince Street is one source of the 100 block becoming known as Captain's Row.

John Fitzgerald Warehouse: 100 South Union Street

The full extent to which the town of Alexandria has encroached into the Potomac River is most amply demonstrated by the Fitzgerald Warehouse. This building, the largest building still standing from Alexandria's earliest decades, is situated on a spot that, according to George Washington's original plan of the streets, was more than a full city block into the watery Potomac. On Washington's survey, King Street ended on the west side of Water (now Lee) Street. The Fitzgerald Warehouse, constructed between 1795 and 1799, sits on the east (river) side of Union Street, more than a block to the east of this point.

John Fitzgerald and a friend, Valentine Peers, arrived from Ireland sometime before the Revolutionary War—some sources speculate 1769—and set up trade in Irish linen. During the Revolutionary War, Fitzgerald suspended the business and served as one of George Washington's Aides-de-Camp. In 1778, Fitzgerald and Peers, also returning from duty in the Revolutionary War, teamed up to purchase a lot on King

The Fitzgerald Warehouse, *photographed in 1955. At that time, the warehouse housed the Old Sailors Inn, which remained in this location until 1996. (Alexandria Library Special Collection)*

Street between Fairfax and Water Streets and the rights to the mudflats to the east of that property. The lot was purchased from the Patterson family, who had in turn earlier purchased it from the estate of Lawrence Washington (George Washington's half-brother) in 1752; the mudflats were purchased directly from the city.

In 1781, for reasons not clear, the partnership was dissolved and Fitzgerald retained the sole rights to the lot and waterfront. Work raising the mudflats with soil from above the bluff had already begun, and continued until 1786, when there is record of Fitzgerald leasing access to this land to other merchants, although without any apparent building on the lot. A decade later, the warehouse as currently constructed was built.

John Fitzgerald died on December 2, 1799, within two weeks of his close friend and business partner George Washington. The Fitzgerald Warehouse is still one of Alexandria's finest structures, worthy of its central location at the primary commercial intersection of the seafaring town.

The building passed through many owners, uses, and adventures, including a Supreme Court review of its ownership in 1850. It survived plundering by British Forces in the War of 1812, recovered and garnered substantial business from the rail lines that traversed Union Street before the Civil War, then once again experienced—and survived—plundering, this time by Union Forces during the Civil War. Today it has a more peaceful existence as an office building with shops on the ground floor.

Carlyle House: 121 North Fairfax Street
The Carlyle House is the grandest structure in the city, and it is hard to imagine this house as contemporary with the more humble houses nearby built by Washington, Ramsay, and Dalton—but it was. In 1741, at age twenty-one, Scottish merchant John Carlyle settled in the area that became Alexandria to serve as the colonial agent for a British merchant and exporter. His financial fortunes soared both through his own mercantile operations and through his marriage to Sarah Fairfax, cousin of the Sixth Lord Cameron of Fairfax, the largest landholder in the area. The Carlyle House is Alexandria's only stone structure dating from the eighteenth century.

After the charter and survey of Alexandria, Carlyle purchased two lots in the 1749 auction. These lots, situated between the location designated for the city government and the Potomac, were ideal for a merchant with political ambitions. By 1749, Carlyle had amassed a financial empire that included several plantations around Virginia, a foundry, mills, and a trading network that spanned the US Colonies, West Indies, and Europe. He was also a founding trustee of the city.

When Carlyle set about building his home in Alexandria, from 1749 to 1753, he scaled the building to suit his stature. So it was natural that, on the eve of the French and Indian War,

The façade of the Carlyle House *just before restoration in 1976 (Alexandria Library Special Collection)*

British General Braddock, also a Scot and recent arrival, would choose this house as his political and military base of operations (*see page 7*). At the start of that war, Carlyle was appointed Commissary of the Virginia Forces, both leveraging and furthering his financial empire.

Sarah died in 1761, and John Carlyle later married Sybil West, sister of John West Jr. (*see page 39*). John Carlyle lived in this house until his death in 1780, passing the house to his son George Carlyle, who died shortly thereafter. The house then passed to John Carlyle Herbert, John senior's grandson, through his daughter Sarah. John sold the house in 1827.

As befit a prominent family, and due to the scale of the house and the extent of the grounds, the Carlyle House was built well back from the street, allowing gardens and walks to surround the house. Unfortunately, after the house passed from the Carlyle family, the open space in front of the house allowed another structure to be built between the house and the street, obscuring it from view. For nearly a century and a half, the house was completely obscured by the Mansion House Hotel (*see photo, page 111*). After the Civil War the hotel and the Carlyle House became derelict until the house was obtained by the Northern Virginia Regional Park Authority in 1970. The house and grounds were restored and opened to the public in 1976.

A sketch of the Carlyle House *which appeared in* Harpers New Monthly *magazine, 1880. (Alexandria Library Special Collection)*

Lawrason House:
301 South Saint Asaph Street
Shreve & Lawrason Warehouse:
100 Prince Street
Fowle House:
711 Prince Street

James and Alice Lawrason arrived in Alexandria between 1790 and 1795 from Canada, with their son Thomas, who had been born in 1780. Shortly after arrival in Alexandria, James established a trading company to import and export wares with partner Benjamin Shreve. Shreve, born in 1747 in New Jersey, at the time had one child, a son of the same name, born in Alexandria in 1772. Little else is recorded about the Shreve family.

In 1799, Lawrason and Shreve purchased a plot of land on the southeast corner of Duke and Saint Asaph Streets, including what is now 301 South Saint Asaph Street, through a series of transactions and intermediaries, from the executors of John Alexander's estate—the same John Alexander family that owned the land upon which Alexandria was founded.

The lot was divided and the Lawrason family built, on the northern half of this property, one of Alexandria's finest structures at the time, now number 301. The brick structure, still a private residence today, includes a widow's walk from which the operations of the family's wharf could be easily seen, and which could itself be seen from far below on the Potomac River. The other half of the property, slightly farther south and across a jointly owned alley, was eventually built on by the heirs of Benjamin Shreve, who died in 1801.

The Shreve & Lawrason Company constructed the warehouse at the bottom of Prince Street in 1810. Like most buildings along what is now Union Street, this land was reclaimed from the Potomac by leveling the bluff above the waterfront. During the ensuing decades this facility saw the import of household goods, rum and wine, and food such as cheese, salmon, sugar, and salt pork. Later, in the nineteenth century it was used for industrial products, grain, and hides.

James Lawrason's son Thomas established the Lawrason & Fowle shipping company with partner William Fowle, who had moved to Alexandria from Boston in 1800; Lawrason & Fowle became one of Alexandria's most prominent shipping lines in the early 1800s. Thomas Lawrason died prematurely in 1819, leaving his wife Elizabeth and five young children residing in the house on South Saint Asaph Street. Elizabeth Lawrason never remarried, and eventually moved to New Orleans after her youngest son had established himself there. Shortly before her departure in 1824, during the Marquis de Lafayette's state visit to Alexandria (*see page 25*), the widow Elizabeth opened her grand home to Lafayette, who resided there for the duration of his visit to the city.

Flounder Houses

Flounder houses gained their name due to their resemblance to the fish: flat and without windows or doors on one side, often attached to a neighboring home like a flounder lying on the seabed, and with all the windows, doors, and architectural detail on the other side. Because these houses resemble one-half a house, local lore states that they were constructed with the intent of building the other half later. Beginning and then stopping construction is said to be either due to a rush to build on the property to meet the land auction's terms that required building a home within two years of purchase of the lot, or that the owner did not yet own the adjoining lot.

More likely, this architectural style simply allowed the builder to construct the home against an already-present home with minimal effort. The pitched roof allowed improved water drainage off the residential lot in an era when streets were often muddy or flooded. Flounder houses are also a notable architectural presence in Philadelphia, a city with which Alexandria shared much commerce and politics as well as architectural style during the last decades of Colonial rule.

Many flounder houses exist throughout the old section of Alexandria, including 208 Duke Street, 514 South Fairfax Street, 315 and 321 South Saint Asaph Street, and 324 South Royal Street.

208 Duke Street, *one of the original flounder houses in Alexandria, built in 1775. The photograph is undated. (Alexandria Library Special Collection)*

William Fowle went on to build the shipping line into one of the mid-Atlantic's largest, eventually changing the name to William Fowle & Co. Included in his business was the commissioning and launch of the 500-ton ship *Alexandria* in 1836. He also built the striking Georgian mansion at 711 Prince Street in 1815, and over time purchased neighboring lots until the garden comprised most of the block to King and Washington. The Fowle family lived in that residence until 1969.

Robert Townsend Hooe House: 201 South Lee Street

Robert Townsend Hooe was born in 1743 in Charles County, Maryland, and served as an officer in the 12th Maryland Battalion during the Revolutionary War. He arrived in Alexandria shortly after the war and proved to be one of its most industrious inhabitants. By 1780 he had built this structure—one of the largest and most visible in the small town—and acquired a number of other lots throughout the town. He built a warehouse and wharf at the corner of Union and Duke Streets (with his partner Richard Howson), and became the first mayor of Alexandria (1780-1781). Hooe was also a founding director of the Bank of Alexandria (*see page 78*), alongside George Washington. Later, Hooe was one of the justices appointed by James Madison, an act that eventually led to the Marbury vs. Madison case before the Supreme Court. Hooe, along with Dennis

Knowing that you have a vessel bound to some port in Spain, I am inclined to ask if it is safe and practicable to bring from thence a good Jack Ass, to breed from.

George Washington, in a letter to Robert Hooe, 1784.

Ramsay and William Harper, were the three Alexandria plaintiffs against James Madison.

The building left the Hooe family shortly after his death. It next served as a bank and over time had a number of commercial and industrial uses. It returned to private residence in 1919 as two houses, and in 2005 the residences were reunited into a single home.

The Robert Townsend Hooe House, *photographed in 1936. At the time, the entrance on Lee Street and the entrance on Prince Street gave access to two separate houses. The house was reunited into one residence in 2005. (Alexandria Library Special Collection)*

Captain's Row and Gentry Row:
the 100 and 200 blocks of Prince Street

Captain's Row, covering the 100 block of Prince Street, gets its name from the popular belief that the these houses were built primarily by sea captains and owners of shipping lines wishing to reside near their shops, docks, and cargo. Similarly, Gentry Row, on the 200 block of Prince Street, is so named due to the picturesque nature of the houses that line it.

Both of these streets are most closely identified with Captain John Harper, who was born in 1728 in Philadelphia. Harper had previously developed a successful shipping and merchant business in Philadelphia with business partner William Hartshorn. Harper move to Alexandria in 1772 or 1773 with his wife, Sarah, leaving Hartshorn to tend the business in Philadelphia. Captain Harper settled at 207 Prince Street, (*see Fairfax House, page 50*) and thereafter purchased the lots and built the houses at 209, 211, and 213 Prince Street. About this time he also purchased all of the land on the north side of the street in one lot, and divided the purchase into smaller lots and sold them individually

John Harper died in 1804. The majority of the structures on the 100 block of Prince Street were destroyed by fire in 1827; most of the houses on this block date to the period of rebuilding immediately thereafter.

Captain Harper's son, William Harper, served with George Washington during the Revolutionary War, and was one of the justices who brought the Marbury vs. Madison lawsuit to the Supreme Court.

The north side of the 100 block of Prince Street, *known as Captain's Row, photographed in 1925. All the houses shown in this photo still exist. The warehouse at the bottom of the hill is the Shreve & Lawrason Warehouse. (Alexandria Library Special Collection)*

The Robert E. Lee Boyhood Home: 607 Oronoco Street

This house was constructed in 1795 by John Potts, a prominent local businessman, and sold shortly thereafter to William Fitzhugh. Fitzhugh was among the most prominent Virginians of the era: He was a member of the Continental Congress, member of the Virginia House of Delegates, and Virginia state senator. Because of their status and influence in Virginia colonial and state politics, Fitzhugh and George Washington were well acquainted.

In 1783, Harry Lee settled in Alexandria with his first wife, Matilda Ludwell, whom he had married at Stratford Hall, the Lee family ancestral home in Westmoreland County, Virginia. From this base, in the ensuing decade he traveled extensively, often accompanied by his family, continuing his career as an officer, delegate to the Continental Congress, governor of Virginia, and member of the US House of Representatives.

In the first decade of the 1800s, a series of financial failures caused Harry Lee to lose most of his assets and be forced into debtor's prison in 1810. Upon release, he returned his family, including his son Robert E. Lee and four other children, to Alexandria, renting the house at 611 Cameron Street. In 1811, he moved his family, including a new sixth child, to the house at 607 Oronoco, renting from William Fitzhugh, to be nearer to the rest of the Lee family. It was here that Robert

E. Lee was to spend the most stable and enjoyable parts of his childhood, although largely without his father. In 1812, Harry Lee sustained debilitating injuries trying to contain a riot in Baltimore and thereafter traveled alone to the West Indies to seek more favorable weather. Harry Lee's second wife, Anne Carter Lee, moved the family briefly to 407 North Washington Street in 1817 but returned to 607 Oronoco Street in 1821. Harry never recovered and died on the return journey from the West Indies, in Georgia in 1818, when Robert was eleven years old. Harry and Robert had spent only about five years together; as an adult Robert E. Lee rarely spoke of his father. After Harry's death, Anne raised their six children mainly through the generosity of the Fitzhugh and Lee families in the area.

William Fitzhugh served as Robert E. Lee's mentor and patron, including petitioning Secretary of War John Calhoun recommending Robert be admitted to West Point. Robert E. Lee eventually married Mary Custis, granddaughter of William Fitzhugh and great granddaughter of Martha Washington by her first marriage. Lee entered West Point in 1825 and returned to this home occasionally thereafter. Anne Carter Lee died in 1829, and the house returned to use by the Fitzhughs.

The house served as a museum dedicated to the Lee family for many years. In 2000, it was purchased and returned to use as a private residence.

The Lee Brothers Arrive in Alexandria

The Lee Family for many years served as one of Alexandria's patrician families, with a historical role in the city equal to that of the Washington family. The Lee family's most prominent members, including Revolutionary War General "Light Horse Harry" Lee (1756-1818) and Attorney General Charles Lee (1758-1818) adopted the town as their home and surrounded themselves with family, providing Alexandria a legacy that was to last for several generations.

Ultimately four Lee brothers, General "Harry" Lee, Charles Lee, Richard Bland Lee, and Edmund Jennings Lee, were to settle in Alexandria. From the first arrival in the 1780s until the early nineteenth century, the town saw the settlement and birth of many members of the extended Lee family. At their highest number, around 1815, about thirty members of the Lee family lived in Alexandria, primarily at the northern end of the town.

The first member of the Lee family to arrive in Alexandria was Charles Lee, who settled in Alexandria in 1782 and went on to serve as US Attorney General under President Washington from 1795 to 1801. Upon his arrival, Charles Lee purchased several lots, including two acres between Oronoco and Pendleton Streets, one half-acre on the corner of Wilkes and South Fairfax Streets, and several acres between Patrick, Fayette, Queen, and Oronoco Streets.

**Site of the Marshall House Hotel:
Corner of King and Pitt Streets**
The southeast corner of Pitt and King Streets claims the distinction of being the location of the first casualty of the American Civil War. On May 24, 1861, on the day that Virginia's secession from the Union became effective, Union troops from the District of Columbia

On his brother Charles' urging, Gen. "Light Horse Harry" Lee, father of Robert E. Lee, settled in Alexandria in 1783, and purchased around twenty lots of land in total. He eventually settled his family on Oronoco Street. From this home, General Lee served as a delegate to the Continental Congress (1786-1788), and Governor of Virginia (1791-1794).

Edmund Jennings Lee (1772-1843) arrived in Alexandria shortly after his brothers, after gaining a law degree from Princeton University. Edmund served on the Alexandria City Council and was mayor of the city from 1815 to 1818. He died in what is now referred to as the Lee-Fendall House in 1843.

Richard Bland Lee (1761-1827), the fourth of the four brothers to settle in Alexandria, arrived in 1811, after spending the majority of his life at Sully Plantation in Fairfax County. Richard later resettled to Fairfax County, and then to his final home at 6th and N Streets, in Southwest Washington, DC.

In addition to the Robert E. Lee Boyhood Home at 607 Oronoco Street (see page 66), also in Alexandria are the Lee-Fendell House at 614 Oronoco Street, which is open to the public, the Lee-Hopkins House at 609 Oronoco Street, the Charles Lee House at 407 North Washington Street, and the Hodgson House (William Hodgson married Portia Lee, cousin to the Lee brothers, in 1799) at 207 Prince. Charles Lee also resided for a brief time at 220 North Washington Street; "Light Horse Harry" Lee and his family resided at 611 Cameron Street from 1810 to 1811.

crossed the Potomac and seized the city, both as a preemptive defensive act and to secure the port and rail infrastructure for use by Union forces.

James W. Jackson, who owned the Marshall House Hotel, had been flying the Confederate flag from the roof of the hotel with the intent that it would be visible from the District. Col. Elmer Ellsworth of the Union forces entered the hotel on the morning of the occupation in order to take down the flag. After Ellsworth had removed the flag and was descending the hotel's main staircase, Jackson shot Ellsworth. Union troops accompanying Ellsworth returned fire and Jackson was fatally shot.

The Marshall House Hotel, like many other buildings in Alexandria, was quickly taken over by Union forces to serve as a hospital and offices in support of the war effort. The building became a hotel once again after the war, under different ownership, and was for a while a prominent tourist attraction made famous by the skirmish between Ellsworth and Jackson.

The original building was torn down in the 1950s.

The site is marked by a plaque that is somewhat biasedin its description of these events, mentioning the death of Confederate sympathizer Jackson but not the death of Union Col. Ellsworth.

James Green's Furniture Factory: 200 South Fairfax Street

Green's Furniture Factory, located at the corner of South Fairfax Street and Prince Street, is one of the most substantial buildings in historic Alexandria. In 1817, William Green, a British cabinetmaker, came to Alexandria and sought to continue his trade in the town. During William's lifetime, he worked out of a number of locations in Alexandria. According

Spite Houses

"Spite houses" gained that name due to the popular notion that these small residences were built to resolve disputes over the use or ownership of the alleys that were common in the early years of the town, and still visible in some blocks today. According to local folklore, the owner of a house on one side of the alley would simply build on to his own house, often said to occur "overnight," to eliminate the ability of the homeowner of the house on the other side of the alley to use, and presumably abuse, that alley. In truth, these houses were more likely simple additions used to house servants or slaves.

The two most notable examples of spite houses in Alexandria are at 523 Queen Street and 403 Prince Street. The house at 403 Prince is known to have been built around 1883, and the external walls of the neighboring houses form the internal side walls of this spite house.

to Kolbe and Greve, archivists at the Virginia Library, William's son James, who had who had learned the trade from his father, purchased a large brick building on this site in 1834. The site had formerly held a grain storage and wholesale business. The Greens repurposed the building, adding a steam engine to drive mechanical mills, lathes, and turning devices.

The facility stayed in the Green family, including with William's son James and grandsons John and Stephen, until its sale in 1887. During this period, Green's Furniture was a significant manufacturer and distributor of furniture throughout the mid-Atlantic. During the Civil War, the building was used briefly as a military prison by Union forces. The building passed through a number of other industrial uses, including a

Victorian Alexandria

While Old Town Alexandria is noted for its outstanding examples of Colonial and Federal architecture, it also contains some gems of the Victorian Era. Victorian architecture, notable for its ornate style and intricate detailing, was popular during the second half of the 1800s, during the latter part of Queen Victoria's rule. In Alexandria, Victorian homes were often built on the few undeveloped residential lots that remained more than 100 years after the original lots were auctioned off, which is why these homes can be found scattered in small groups in a wide arc a few blocks north and south of King Street. Fine examples of Victorian homes are located at 217-229 and 320-326 South Pitt Street, 226-230 North Royal Street, and 509-509½ and 529-535 South Fairfax Street. The two houses at 509 and 509½ South Fairfax were built in 1894 on one existing lot, thus the fractional address. The four houses at 529-535 South Fairfax are notable for their very narrow design; each is about 11 feet wide.

car dealership in the mid 1900s, until being renovated into residences in 1976.

The external brick walls are original to the early-nineteenth century building. James Green's initials are still visible on the metal supporting rods on the south end of the Fairfax Street façade.

Friedson's Grocery Store:
300 South Fairfax Street
This building, now a private residence, was an important feature in the Hayti neighborhood of free blacks that came into existence around 1810. The current structure was built in 1840, and there is evidence of ownership by a free black family as far back as 1810 and possibly

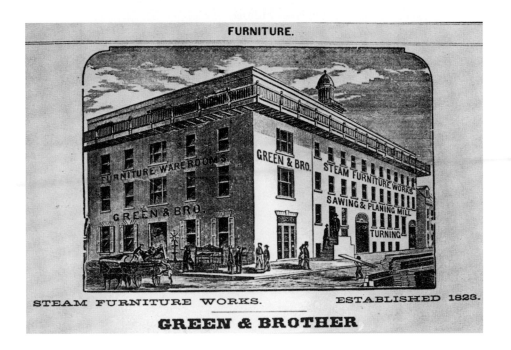

FURNITURE.

GREEN & BRO.

FURNITURE WAREROOMS.
GREEN & BRO.
STEAM FURNITURE WORKS
SAWING & PLANING MILL
TURNING

STEAM FURNITURE WORKS.   ESTABLISHED 1823.

GREEN & BROTHER

as early as 1790. An 1885 historical map of the city shows a grocery store on this location. The structure still displays the original shop windows. It was known as Friedson's Grocery Store until its closure and sale in 1957.

An advertisement for the **James Green Furniture Factory,** *around 1860. (Library of Congress)*

Mutual Ice Company Distribution Building: 110 South Lee Street

Between 1900 and 1930, before the advent of electrical refrigeration, ice houses and ice carts were a common scene in Alexandria, providing the means to cool the iceboxes of Alexandria residents. At the height of the era, about twenty ice wagons from several ice companies worked the streets of Alexandria, delivering ice in thirty-five-pound blocks to

Hayti

Alexandria, which was a part of the District of Columbia from 1801 to 1847, was consequently a "free territory" and a destination and home for many free blacks. Around 1800, the first neighborhoods consisting primarily of free African-Americans began to appear in Alexandria, initially in the area southwest of the intersection of Washington and Duke Streets, known as "the Bottoms." Soon thereafter, around 1810, the area around the intersections of Wolfe Street with Fairfax and Royal Streets began to attract more wealthy African-Americans, including Moses Hepburn, a prominent land developer. Moses' aunt, Anna Jackson, purchased the property at 406 and 408 South Royal in 1820 from Quaker abolitionist Mordecai Miller. The current buildings on these lots date from the 1830s. George Seaton, a prominent African-American abolitionist with an active trade as a master carpenter, built the house at 323 South St. Asaph Street in 1852, and acquired the house at 404 South Royal Street in 1866 as his residence. Seaton was elected to the Virginia House of Delegates in 1869. The home remained in the Seaton family until 1927. At its greatest extent, Hayti encompassed the area from South Pitt Street to South Fairfax Street, and from Prince Street to Wilkes Street.

businesses and households roughly every other day.

In 1900 William Reardon and J.W. Hammond joined forces to establish the Mutual Ice Company in Alexandria. By 1920, they had two ice plants, one at the corner of Union and Cameron, and a larger one north of town at 1200 North Henry Street. The second plant could manufacture sixty thousand tons of ice annually. The Mutual Ice Company also established locations around Alexandria to support the cutting, storage, delivery, and sale of ice; the building at 110 South Lee Street served as one of these delivery stations. Stables and a wagon repair facility existed in the alley behind the current building.

The Mutual Ice Company closed in 1937 as electricity became more common. The building was used for many years by a wholesale fruit distributor and is now home to an architectural firm.

Gadsby's Tavern: 134 North Royal Street
In the first decade of the 1800s, this site, now a restaurant and museum, contained one of the most luxurious taverns and boarding houses in the United States. John Gadsby, an English immigrant and hotelier, rented the building in 1794 and for the subsequent 17 years created the most prominent hotel in the area. At the height of its existence in the area's cultural and political scene, it included seven buildings spread across a half acre bordered by Cameron, King, Royal, and Pitt Streets. What is now Gadsby's Tavern Museum is actually two of these buildings. The larger, to the north, was built by Alexandrian John Wise in 1793 to expand upon the smaller building, which he had purchased a year earlier.

During the period when the tavern was managed by John Gadsby, the complex hosted balls, plays, and inaugural events for several presidents, including Thomas Jefferson's Inaugural Ball. During a particularly raucous inaugural evening in Washington, DC, newly elected President Andrew Jackson slipped out of the White House and walked the 10 miles to Alexandria to spend a quiet night at Gadsby's Tavern. James Madison, John Quincy Adams, and the Marquis de Lafayette also were guests of the tavern. At the end of George Washington's tenure as president, the tavern hosted a banquet in his honor to welcome the Alexandrian home.

After Gadsby's departure, the tavern continued to operate until the Civil War, when it served a variety of uses at the discretion of the Union army. After that war, the tavern's fate followed Alexandria's trajectory downward, and it stood derelict for many decades. In the 1910s and 1920s, various features were removed and sold, including the ballroom interior to the Metropolitan Museum of Art in New York. The city later purchased the building, then renovated and restored it. Gadsby's Tavern Museum opened as a museum and restaurant in 1976.

Stabler-Leadbeater Apothecary: 105 & 107 South Fairfax Street

This remarkable shop, the precursor to the modern pharmacy, was in continuous use as an apothecary by the same family for nearly a century and half, from its founding in 1792 to its closure in 1933.

The building itself was built by a coppersmith, roughly ten years before Edward Stabler, who had finished his apprenticeship in Leesburg, rented it and established his business there in 1792. As an apothecary, Stabler sold not only medicines but perfumes,

dental and medical equipment, and other toiletries. The medicines were mixed in the shop using ingredients purchased and imported from around the world. The early business was successful, serving the town on a near-monopoly basis, and in the 1830s had expanded to include ownership of both 105 and 107 South Fairfax streets and other miscellaneous buildings, including, for a while, the Athenaeum (*see page 86*) for storage and supply for the wholesale business.

In 1831 Edward Stabler died, leaving the business to his son, William Stabler. The business continued to prosper, and by William's death in 1852 it employed William's two brothers and his brother-in-law, John Leadbeater. Leadbeater bought out the

The Stabler-Leadbeater Apothecary, *in a photograph dated 1890. The City of Alexandria had just completed electrification. (Alexandria Library Special Collection)*

remaining Stabler family interests by 1860. During the Civil War, the business supplied Union troops and the many Union hospitals and surgeries in the city. By 1865, the business became the primary wholesaler of apothecary supplies in the region, offering goods through the two buildings on Fairfax Street, one on King Street, one in Washington DC, and various warehouses, augmented by twelve salesmen who offered goods from North Carolina to West Virginia.

The traditionally-run business failed to anticipate the industrialization of the supply of pharmaceutical and household goods in the early decades of the twentieth century, and went bankrupt in 1933. The building, whose interior had remained largely unchanged since its founding, was the oldest pharmacy in the United States at the time, and was quickly recognized for its historic value. Shortly after closure, it was purchased at auction by Landmark Society of Alexandria, which was formed to preserve the building and care for its collection. The structure reopened as a museum in 1939 with much of the contents, including supplies and natural chemicals still in place. It was updated and renovated again in 2006, and is now managed as a museum by the City of Alexandria.

Bank of Alexandria: 133 North Fairfax Street
The Bank of Alexandria Building is the most significant remaining portion of a series of related buildings that once fronted the length of the 100 block of North Fairfax

An Aerial view of the intersection of King and Union Streets, *1935. Note the Strand in the foreground, and compare this photo to a similar one taken seventy years earlier in 1865 (on page 20). The shoreline is significantly altered, particularly on the right side of this photo, where the land has been extended into the water and the wooden building, formerly the Old Dominion Boat Club, has been added. The Ramsay Warehouse at 101 King Street is clearly visible, and the pitched roof of the former John Fitzgerald Warehouse is apparent on the left side of the photo. The Torpedo Factory, a relative newcomer, is on the right, apparently busy with many cars parked outside (Alexandria Library Special Collection).*

Street, obscuring the Carlyle House from view. This building was constructed in 1807 for the Bank of Alexandria, which had been chartered fifteen years earlier and had operated out of 305 Cameron, a short distance away. Historians Smith and Miller state that George Washington owned twenty five shares of the bank, purchased for $5,000. Upon Washington's death, these shares were bequeathed to the Alexandria Academy (*see photo on page 22*).

The Bank of Alexandria failed in 1834, during Andrew Jackson's presidency, an early casualty of Jackson's war on banks and the panic and deep recession that followed. The building was purchased shortly thereafter by James Green and incorporated into Green's Mansion House Hotel immediately to the south.

Both the hotel and the bank building were occupied by Union forces during the Civil War, and used as a hospital and offices. After the war, the former Bank of Alexandria and Mansion House Hotel buildings returned to use as a hotel and eventually private residences. During the restoration of the Carlyle House in 1976, the former Green's Mansion House Hotel building was demolished. After additional research into the bank building, it was decided the save the bank structure due to its heritage and authentic interior, much of which dates to its original construction. The Bank of Alexandria Building is now privately owned.

Chapter v
Religious and
Cultural Institutions

Christ Church Alexandria: 114 North Washington Street

Construction of Christ Church Alexandria, which took about five years, was completed in 1773. As with the Old Presbyterian Meeting House, John Carlyle was the major funder of construction costs of the original church building. James Wren, one of the most prolific and influential architects in Colonial Virginia in the Revolutionary period, designed the building.

The church's original deed of land included a larger area than is evident today. Originally, the property extended northward well beyond the current lay of Cameron Street, and west beyond Columbus Street. This original plot, larger than a city block, allowed the church itself to be placed in the path of Cameron Street between Washington and Columbus Streets, and caused Old Town's only change from the town's original street plan. Because the area north of the church, through which Cameron now runs, was used in the first decades of the church as a burial ground, the struggles between the city and the church on the construction of Cameron Street were difficult and protracted, lasting nearly a half century. The conflict was resolved in 1816 when the church allowed the street to be constructed in its current path and the gravesites moved.

Christ Church was the home parish of the Lee family, including "Light Horse Harry" Lee and Robert E. Lee, and of the Washington family. During the early years of the church, pews were leased by donation; both the Lee and Washington pews are now marked. The Washington pew retains its original horseshoe shape, constructed in this

Christ Church,
photographed in 1901, from the corner of Cameron and Columbus Streets (Library of Congress)

manner so that in the wintertime families could share, under blankets covering their legs, the coal heaters they brought from home.

It has become a tradition for sitting presidents to visit Christ Church sometime during their tenure, often around George Washington's birthday. Franklin Roosevelt and Winston Churchill worshipped at the church on January 1, 1942.

Old Presbyterian Meeting House: 321 South Fairfax Street

The Old Presbyterian Meeting House, along with Christ Church, was among Alexandria's first congregations and served as the primary religious establishments in the city for many decades. They continue to be active parishes central to the life of Old Town Alexandria. The original Old Presbyterian Meeting House was built at approximately the same time and with the same floor plan as Christ Church.

The original Old Presbyterian Meeting House building was constructed in 1775 on land purchased by Minister Richard Thom for one shilling two years earlier. A short time later, John Carlyle and William Ramsay funded an advertisement in the Alexandria newspaper for bids to construct the building.

The current building, which was constructed after a fire destroyed the original, dates to 1835. The bell tower, which appears unfinished but which was built according to design, was added in 1843. The bucolic graveyard behind the building is the home of The Grave of the Unknown Soldier of the Revolutionary War and the gravesite of John and Sara Carlyle and other historical Alexandria figures.

The Old Presbyterian Meeting House was the site of George Washington's memorial services, held on December 30, 1799, after the Meeting House bell had been rung in mourning for four continuous days. The services lasted two days due the number of speakers, and was presided over jointly by the rectors of the Old Presbyterian Meeting House, Christ Church, and a more recently established Methodist Church.

The Lyceum: 201 South Washington Street
In the early part of the nineteenth century, the growing European movement of societies for investigating and debating scientific and cultural phenomenon came to America in the form of the Lyceum Movement. In England, for example, the Royal Society, Royal Geographic Society, and many other more local versions of these had provided the space and organization for intellectuals and the public to come together, witness experiments, and debate the nature of the physical and philosophical sciences. In the early 1800s, these societies gained popularity and were a

significant part of the intellectual growth of the Victorian era on both sides of the Atlantic.

In America, Josiah Holbrook, a journeyman teacher, founded the Lyceum Movement; the first Lyceum opened in 1826 in Millbury, Massachusetts. The Alexandria Lyceum was founded by Benjamin Hallowell, a Quaker teacher who had arrived in Alexandria in 1824 from Philadelphia to establish a private boarding school on the Quaker model.

According to Lewis Winston, Hallowell rented a residence from the Hooe family and quickly established his school by the end of that year. The Hallowell School would go on to educate the children of many prominent Alexandrians, including Robert E. Lee as he prepared to enter West Point.

During his time in Alexandria, Hallowell offered lectures to the general public on scientific topics. At the school, these discussions were so popular that Hallowell, with the assistance of friends around Alexandria, created the Lyceum Society in 1834. In 1839 the Lyceum Society built the current building funded by subscriptions from the general public. In 1842, due to declining health and the stresses of running an ever-growing school, Hallowell purchased a farm in Fauquier County, Virginia, and relocated there, handing the school to his nephews and the society to his colleagues.

The building was taken over by Union forces during the Civil War. After the war, it became a private residence and then, in 1938, an office building. The Lyceum is now owned by the City of Alexandria and serves as the city's historical museum and functions once again as a center for educational lectures.

The Athenaeum: 201 Prince Street
The Athenaeum, situated between Captain's Row and Gentry Row on Prince Street, was originally constructed to house the Bank of the Old Dominion in 1851. It served that purpose until the Civil War, when the bank closed and the building was repurposed by Union forces to house the US Commissary Quartermaster. After the Civil War, in 1870, it housed the renamed First Virginia Bank until 1907, when it was purchased by the Stabler-Leadbeater Apothecary and used as a warehouse and distribution center for their wholesale business.

The First Free Methodist Church of Alexandria purchased the building in 1925; Alexandrians worshipped at this site until 1964, when it was sold to the Northern Virginia Fine Arts Association. This association continues to use the building as an exhibit space for art, concert hall, and meeting center.

Free Methodist Church: 424 South Lee Street
Nationally, the Free Methodist Church movement was started in 1860, in Pekin, New York, as an abolitionist offshoot of the national Methodist Church. In Alexandria, the First Free Methodist Church was founded in 1880 on the edge of the Hayti neighborhood of free blacks. The building was built by

The Athenaeum *at 201 Prince Street, photographed in 1936 (Alexandria Library Special Collection)*

brothers George and Lewis Peverill and Samuel English. English donated the land; the Peverill brothers arranged for the manpower and materials necessary for the construction. As the racially integrated congregation grew and became successful, it eventually needed to find less restrictive facilities and in 1925 purchased the building that housed the First Virginia Bank, now known as The Athenaeum. The congregation stayed at that site until 1963, when it moved to its current location in western Alexandria. The Lee Street building is now a private residence.

Alexandria Contraband and Freedman's Cemetery: 1001 South Washington Street

During the Civil War, the city of Alexandria became the destination for thousands of free blacks and escaped slaves, seeking the protection of Union forces and the anti-slavery laws of the Union. During this period, Alexandria's African-American population was at its peak, comprising about 60 percent of the town's inhabitants. It is a testament to the strength of this migratory force that during the five short years this cemetery was in use, from 1864 to 1869, approximately 1,800 African-Americans were interred, about one per day on average.

Those of African descent arrived in Alexandria not only out of a desire for freedom, but also with a need for the basic health care and subsistence that their earlier lives had lacked. Disease was common among those who arrived. In 1864, the Superintendent of Contrabands, as freed blacks were commonly known, ordered a separate gravesite be designated at the southern end of the town for these free African-Americans.

After the conclusion of the Civil War, the cemetery was no longer used and was eventually forgotten. In subsequent decades, the location was used as a rail yard, a gas station, and a small office building. In the 1980s, driven by the Alexandria Historical Office and the initiation of plans to rebuild and reroute the Woodrow Wilson Bridge, the importance of the burial ground was recognized. Local community groups were formed to reclaim the historical ground as a park and memorial. These groups were successful, and the park, dedicated to the memory of those seeking freedom and protection in Alexandria, opened in 2014.

Franklin and Armfield Slave Company (now the Freedom Museum): 1315 Duke Street

This site, along with the Alexandria Contraband and Freedman's Cemetery, offers testimony to the importance of the slave trade – and African-Americans – to the history of the city of Alexandria. The Franklin and Armfield Slave Company was one of three slave trading companies with facilities in Alexandria, and one of the first to recognize the possibility of exporting slaves from Virginia and neighboring states to the

The slave pen at 1315 Duke Street. *After being sold by Franklin and Armfield in 1840, it changed hands several times but remained a slave-trading company. The final owners to use the property in this manner were Price, Birch & Co., pictured here, after the arrival of the Union Army in 1865. (Alexandria Library Special Collection)*

Deep South, driven by the prohibition of the import of slaves enacted in 1808. Several historians note that at its peak, Franklin and Armfield transferred more than 1,000 slaves each year, gathering them in the pens behind the building on Duke Street and transporting them to Natchez and New Orleans either by forced march or on one of the company's three ships. Isaac Franklin managed the facility and the sale of slaves in Natchez and New Orleans; John Armfield managed the business in Alexandria.

The building at Duke Street was built in 1812 (1816 in some sources) as a residence for Gen. Andrew Young. Franklin and Armfield purchased the property in 1828. For the next twelve years, Franklin and Armfield grew to be one of the largest slave companies in the country, earning profits of around $100,000 per year. It is estimated that between 1808 and the start of the Civil War, almost three-quarters of a million slaves were transported from north to south by Franklin and Armfield and other similar companies operating in this manner.

Franklin and Armfield sold the property in 1840 to another slave trading company. It changed hands several more times and, when the Union Army entered Alexandria at the beginning of the Civil War, it was no longer in apparent use. The Union forces used it as a detention center for deserters from the Union Army. The holding areas in the back of the property were demolished in 1870. The building passed through a number of other uses, including hospital, apartment building, and offices. In 1996, the Freedom Museum was established on this site.

An aerial view of Old Town Alexandria looking up King Street, *taken 1935. The George Washington Masonic National Memorial, completed in 1932, dominates the background of the photo. On the right side, the steeples of City Hall and Christ Church are clearly evident. (Library of Congress)*

Chapter VI
Infrastructure

In the city's first hundred years, Alexandria's waterfront moved east, reclaiming an area that was once in the Potomac. Originally, when Fairfax Street was intended as the main north-south street running along the river, Water (now Lee) Street was an incomplete and muddy thoroughfare along the waterfront, interrupted by inlets and busy with the workings of shipping cargo. The construction of piers and the reclamation of land, both intentionally and through siltage of the docks, eventually allowed Water Street to run contiguously along the city waterfront, and later to be superseded by Union Street as the waterfront thoroughfare. This evolution can be best seen at Lee Street Park, between Wilkes and Gibbon, where the bluff is clearly visible. Below this bluff, schooners plied tobacco, slaves, and other wares. Later on, trains crisscrossed the historic district, connecting Alexandria to the growing country. The heart of this area is now a neighborhood playground and sports field.

Alexandria Canal: Canal Center Plaza, Montgomery Street at the Potomac River
During the nineteenth century, Alexandria established itself as a major center for shipping and commerce for the young republic. During this period, shipment of goods by sea was augmented by an expanding web of canals and rails throughout the United States. Alexandria's one canal, conceived as a spur to the Chesapeake and Ohio Canal running from Cumberland, Maryland, to Washington, D.C., was conceived in 1833 and completed ten years later. The canal included an aqueduct bridge near the current Key Bridge at the Georgetown terminus of the C&O Canal.

The lowest lock of the Alexandria Canal, *where it rejoins the Potomac River at the foot of present-day Montgomery Street. This photo is cited as taken in 1862, during the period from 1861 to 1867 when Union troops occupied the city and managed (and ultimately drained) the canal. The canal operated for approximately fifteen years before the Civil War and twenty years after, closing in 1887. (Library of Congress)*

From there, the Alexandria Canal descended through four locks to the northern end of Alexandria. Use of the canal was abandoned in 1886; its only remnant is the recreated lock at its entry point to the Potomac near the bottom of Montgomery Street at Canal Center Plaza.

**Wilkes Street Tunnel:
200 block of Wilkes Street**
The Orange and Alexandria Railroad, founded in 1848 and whose presence contributed to the demise of the Alexandria Canal, was a central feature of the city during the last half of the nineteenth century. Many Alexandria streets,

The 1100 block of Duke Street *(traveling across the photo) where it intersects with Fayette Street (upward on the left side of the photo), looking north and slightly west, photographed in 1863. The photograph was taken from the top of the rail yard roundhouse that served as the main switching station for Alexandria. The train depot in the foreground has in modern times served as the site of the Fannon gas works, recently redeveloped as Old Town Village. The brick house on Duke Street in the center of the photo remains. (Alexandria Library Special Collection)*

including Union, Wilkes, Washington, Fayette, and Henry, carried rail lines that supported the carriage of a vast array of goods to and from the busy waterfront. Today, the most prominent evidence of this era is the King Street Station, still in use as the main train station for Alexandria, and the Wilkes Street Tunnel, built from 1851 to 1856 at a cost of $20,000. This tunnel, 170 feet long, 15 feet

The Virginia Shipbuilding Company, *the successor to the Hunter Shipyard. The rail line visible in the far right of the photo ran roughly parallel and between Wilkes and Wolfe Streets. This photo is undated but was likely taken between 1930 and 1945.*

wide, and 17 feet tall, enabled ship-borne goods to be carried to rail yards west of town without having to climb the bluff now crested by Lee Street. The tunnel, at the intersection of Wilkes and Fairfax Streets in the residential section of southeast Old Town, is now a pedestrian tunnel and part of the Mount Vernon Trail. The last rails were torn from the streets in and around the tunnel in the 1970s.

Hunter Shipyard: 400-600 South Union Street

Along the shoreline of these two blocks of South Union Street, John Hunter founded Alexandria's largest shipyard in 1783. Hunter and his family owned and ran this shipyard for eighty years until the Civil War, when it was abandoned due to the disruption of trade in the town. The Hunter Shipyard built three- and four-masted schooners that worked the Chesapeake Bay and Atlantic coast, carrying among other items some of the 100,000 hogsheads (barrels) of tobacco that were exported from Alexandria annually.

In 1880 to 1881 the site was purchased by the Potomac Manufacturing Company, which established a large iron foundry on the site. Soon thereafter, the site was purchased by a group of businessmen who established the Virginia Iron Shipbuilding Company. That company also did not last long, and the facility was sold to the Arrow Shipbuilding Company in 1887 (also known as the Arrow Steamship Company in some Alexandria records). Shipbuilding continued on this site under a variety of owners until reaching a new peak in World War I and again in World War II, when shipbuilding and its supporting activities such as iron manufacturing existed from the foot of Duke Street to the now-natural area a few hundred yards north of the Jones Point Lighthouse. Shipbuilding activity faded quickly after this war and the area found other industrial uses; for example, the establishment of a Ford Motor Company parts manufacturing plant at the foot of Gibbon Street. The area is now residential, but pilings and other evidence of this earlier era are plainly visible.

TOUR ONE: Oldest and Finest Alexandria

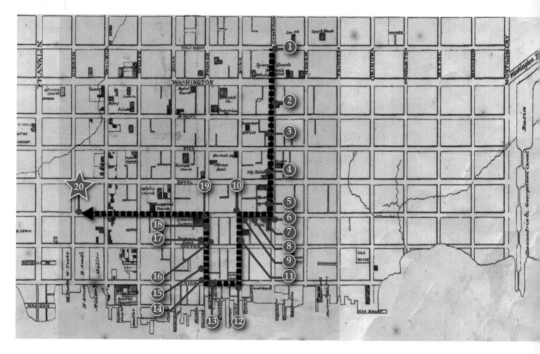

LOCATIONS

1. Christ Church
2. Home of the Ninth Lord Cameron of Fairfax
3. George Washington's Townhouse
4. Gadsby's Tavern
5. City Hall
6. Wise's Tavern
7. Bank of Alexandria
8. Carlyle House
9. Ramsay House
10. Stabler-Leadbeater Apothecary Museum
11. Ramsay Warehouse
12. Fitzgerald Warehouse
13. Fitzhugh Warehouse
14. Shreve & Lawrason Warehouse
15. Captains Row
16. Athenaeum
17. Hooe House
18. Gentry Row
19. Green's Furniture Factory
20. Old Presbyterian Meeting House

Chapter VII
Alexandria Walking Tours

Tour One: Oldest and Finest Alexandria

Tour One provides an overview of the most historically meaningful sites and streets of the Old Town.

Start at **(1) Christ Church** (p. 81) at the intersection of Cameron and Columbus Streets. Check the docent schedule at the church, which is open to the public on most days. Stroll the grounds to find the gravestones (although the bodies are long removed) of Alexandrians as far back as 1775.

Leave the churchyard through the east "1773" gate, cross Washington Street, and continue east (downhill) on Cameron, the original main street of the town as laid out by George Washington. Half a block ahead, at **(2) 607 Cameron Street** (p. 19), was the longtime home of the Ninth Lord Cameron of Fairfax, and one more block ahead is **(3) George Washington's Townhouse** (p. 43) at 508 Cameron. Continue down Cameron Street to **(4) Gadsby's Tavern** (p. 75) near the intersection of Cameron and Royal; note the deep ice well near the corner, originally used to store food. Step inside and stop for lunch or refreshment. At this point, also look back westward toward Christ Church to see how it obstructs Cameron Street, the only departure from Washington's original survey laying out the town.

Proceed one more block east on Cameron Street, passing **(5) City Hall** (p. 3) on your right, to the intersection of Cameron and Fairfax, the original main intersection in Alexandria. Looking around, you can see **(6) Wise's Tavern** (p. 46) and Alexandria City Hall. You will also see the **(7) Bank of Alexandria** (p. 78) and the **(8) Carlyle House** (p. 55) on the south side of Fairfax Street. City Hall's original and more ornate and architecturally interesting façade faces Cameron Street. A much plainer façade faces Market Square. The original building, which served as a town hall and Fairfax County Courthouse, was constructed in the 1750s. In 1817, the western addition, bell tower, and ornate façade were added along Royal Street. On May 19, 1871, the building was almost completely destroyed by fire but rebuilt in close conformity to the original plan (see back cover).

At this point, turn right and walk south on Fairfax until you arrive at the Carlyle House on the left; stop and explore the house and the unique gardens. From here, look across the street for a good view of City Hall and the Market Square adjacent to it. This square served as the original town market; the Saturday Farmers' Market is now considered the oldest continuing farmers' market in America.

A little farther south on Fairfax Street at the intersection of King Street, is the (9) **Ramsay House** (p. 44), now the Alexandria Visitors Center. If you need additional information about services, locations, or opening times, step inside. Cross King Street and continue down South Fairfax Street to the **(10) Stabler-Leadbeater Apothecary Museum** (p. 76).

After you tour the museum, return to King Street. From this point walk east, downhill, on King Street to see the large number of shops occupying buildings all the way to the Potomac, many of which are

A view of the original main façade of City Hall along Cameron Street.
This photograph was taken in 1890. Note the unpaved roads and new electrical towers. The First Virginia Bank building is just visible to the left. (Alexandria Library Special Collection)

original retail buildings and warehouses from Alexandria's earliest days as a seafaring power. In particular, the 100 block of King Street, including the **(11) Ramsay Warehouse** (p. 44) at 101 King, is almost entirely original to the latter half of the 1700s. As you walk down King Street to Union Street, consider that this steady descent was originally a steep bluff, just below Lee Street (originally Water Street); the first generations of Alexandrians carried soil from above the bluff to fill in the shallow flats between shipping wharves to reclaim land and make access to the deep channel in the center of the river easier.

At Union Street turn right. The **(12) Fitzgerald Warehouse** (p. 52) sits on the river side of Union Street at number 100. If you have the time, walk around the warehouse using the Strand and Wales Alley to investigate the antique stone, brick, and woodwork, including the rings used to hold the pulleys that allowed workers to lift freight to the upper stories. This warehouse's muscular stone foundation has withstood innumerable floods. Proceed south on Union Street to Prince Street, to the **(13) Fitzhugh Warehouse** (p. 66) at 125 South Union, connected to the Fitzhugh family, close friends of the Lee Family, and now containing a Christmas shop, and then to the **(14) Shreve & Lawrason Warehouse** (p. 58) on 100 Prince Street. Proceed up Prince Street, through **(15) Captain's Row** (p. 64). At the intersection with Lee Street, if open, enter the **(16) Athenaeum** (p. 86), and admire the stately architecture of the **(17) Hooe House** (p. 62) across the street. Continue up the 200 block of Prince Street, called **(18) Gentry Row** (p. 64), and turn left onto South Fairfax Street, passing **(19) Green's Furniture Factory** (p. 70), and stopping at the **(20) Old Presbyterian Meeting House** (p. 82). Go inside if open, and stroll the small but striking grounds, including the Tomb of the Unknown Soldier of the Revolutionary War.

This tour is over. To continue seeing the most important sites of Alexandria in the latter half of the 1700s, continue by car to Mount Vernon about 10 miles south, or continue with the next tour, below.

Tour Two: The African-American Presence

Tour Two provides an overview of those sites that are most representative of the lives of both slaves and free blacks during the first century and a half of the city, starting in the most central part of the town, progressing through some more modern elements, and ending at the city's most important African-American memorial sites.

Start by walking through **(1) Hayti** (p. 74), as the neighborhood of affluent African-Americans was called in the early 1800s. Start on the 300 block of South Fairfax, proceed south and turn right onto Wolfe Street, and then left onto the 400 Block of South Royal Street. These three blocks represent the central portion of the neighborhood that originally spanned South Pitt to South Fairfax Streets, and from Prince Street to Wilkes Street. Use the adjacent map to guide your explorations.

During your exploration of this area, see the **(2) Free Methodist Church** (p. 86) at 424 South Lee Street and the former **(3) Friedson's** (p. 72) grocery store at 300 South Fairfax Street, both now private residences.

Continue west on Wolfe Street to the intersection of Washington Street, at the 600 block of Wolfe. Slightly off the road is the **(4) Alexandria Academy** (p. 22). Among the various schools that occupied this building were the Alexandria Free School for the children of poor Alexandrians, financed by George Washington. In 1812, a Free School for Colored Children was founded on the same

TOUR TWO: The African-American Presence

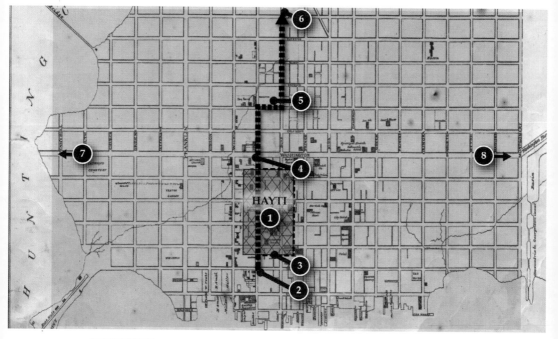

LOCATIONS

1. Hayti
2. Free Methodist Church
3. 300 South Fairfax Street
4. Alexandria Academy
5. Alfred Street Baptist Church
6. Freedom House Museum
7. Alexandria Contraband and Freedman's Cemetery
8. Alexandria Black History Museum

site, financed by prominent African-American Alexandrians.

Continue across Washington Street. A large area on the west side of Washington Street, running north-south from Duke to Franklin and as far west as Patrick Street, was the first neighborhood of free blacks in Alexandria, starting from about 1800. This neighborhood was known as "the Bottoms" due to its low and relatively undesirable land. While few of the original structures from this era remain, the houses facing Washington Street south of Wolfe Street are original and give a sense of the historic architecture.

Continue on Wolfe Street and turn right on Alfred Street. Proceed to 301 Alfred Street, the **(5) Alfred Street Baptist Church** (p. 35). This congregation is Alexandria's oldest African-American Baptist congregation. The congregation started meeting in 1803 and built a church on this lot around 1855. The current building dates to the 1990s. Continue north on Alfred to Duke Street—note the original buildings on the 800 and 900 blocks of Duke Street. Turn left on Duke Street, and continue to the **(6) Freedom Museum** at 1315 Duke Street.

If you wish, proceed to the **(7) Alexandria Contraband and Freedman's Cemetery** (p. 88) at 1001 South Washington Street, or to the **(8) Alexandria Black History Museum,** at 902 Wythe Street.

TOUR THREE: *Alexandria's Waterfront*

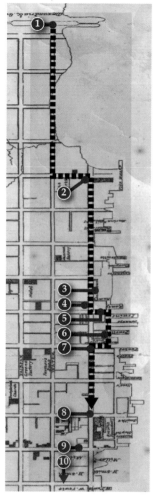

Tour Three: Alexandria's Waterfront

Tour Three provides a selective overview of the waterfront, from north to south, encompassing residential, industrial, and geographic features.

Start at the north end of the Alexandria waterfront at the foot of Montgomery Street, within the modern Canal Center Plaza office complex. Within this complex is a reconstruction of the lowest lock of the **(1) Alexandria Canal** (p. 93).

Walk south, toward town, along the Mount Vernon Trail following the shoreline. For the next 3 blocks, to Pendleton Street and the large warehouse, the shoreline comprises **(2) Oronoco Bay Park,** so named because when the city was laid out the area where Oronoco Street reached the Potomac was the marshy delta of the Oronoco Stream. Continue south past the warehouse and enter **(3) Founders Park** (p. 20) at the corner of Oronoco and Union. At this intersection is the original **(4) West Point**, where Hugh West had his original pier and small warehouse that served as the very first structures of the town, the germination of the trading and seafaring city that followed.

Continue south through Founders Park to the **(5) Torpedo Factory** (p. 79) (100 South Union Street). This building, now a center for the arts, was originally built in 1918 by the

US Navy for the design and manufacture of torpedoes. Although completed too late to contribute to World War I, the plant was very active in World War II, manufacturing the Mark XIV submarine torpedo. After World War II, the complex was used for storage by the federal government until 1969, when the city of Alexandria purchased the building. It took another five years to transform the building; in September 1974, the Torpedo Factory Arts Center opened to the public.

Continue south on Union Street to King Street. On your right, at 101 King Street, is the **(6) Ramsay Warehouse** (p. 44). Diagonally across the intersection is the **(7) Fitzgerald Warehouse** (p. 52). Turn left onto King Street and right immediately onto the Strand, and then right onto Wales Alley to see the Fitzgerald Warehouse from all sides – and also appreciate the land upon which you are walking, the result of manual reclamation of shoreline. Back at Union Street, proceed

A photo of the Alexandria waterfront, *showing the houses along the 500 Block of South Lee Street, in an undated photo. The height and steepness of the hillside above the river is clearly evident. The bluff had long been leveled along most of the Alexandria waterfront decades earlier; this is the only stretch where the original shoreline is evident to this day (Library of Congress).*

south to 100 Prince Street, to the **(8) Shreve & Lawrason Warehouse** (p. 58), which is now a private residence.

Proceed 2 blocks south on Union Street to **(9) Wolfe Street** (p. 24). From shortly after the city's founding until a century ago, this neighborhood was a thriving shipyard. Walk south along Union Street 1 more block. On your left is the narrow Shipyard City Park, and on your right you will see one end of the **(10) Wilkes Street Tunnel**. Together, the pilings in the water at Shipyard Park and the Wilkes Street Tunnel are the last remaining evidence of Alexandria's industrial past.

A little farther on the right on Union Street is Lee Street Park, sometimes referred to as Windmill Hill Park. In this park is the last stretch of the Alexandria waterfront area where the bluff upon which Alexandria was originally laid out still remains visible.

If you like, continue south along the water through Ford's Landing, a residential development on the site of a former Ford automotive plant, and into Jones Point Park, the southernmost end of the historic area. Jones Point Park contains a rich variety of historical markers and exhibits, and the **(11) Jones Point Lighthouse** (p. 97), built in 1855.

Tour Four:
Fun and Quirky Alexandria

This tour presents a winding tour of the historic area, highlighting some of the most historical as well as the most interesting and unusual elements of the town.

Start at **(1) George Washington's Townhouse** (p. 19) at 508 Cameron. In addition to serving as the residence of the founding father while he was in Alexandria, it was the residence of Mick Fleetwood, a founding member of Fleetwood Mac, who lived here and opened a restaurant, Fleetwood's, nearby, in 1994.

Head west, uphill, on Cameron Street and turn left onto Saint Asaph Street, a street named after a Welsh bishop and—indirectly— after a saint about whom no facts are known, and cross over King Street to Prince Street. Turn right on Prince Street to **(2) 605 & 607 Prince**. These houses, built in the 1850s, are the only known examples in Alexandria where the façades of the building, mimicking stone, were originally made of cast iron.

Turn around and proceed east on Prince Street, toward the Potomac River. Pass the fascinating **(3) J. D. Brown House** (p. 48), one of the least changed houses from the first years of the village, on the left.

Turn left on Pitt Street and then right on King Street, and look for the marker signifying the first shots of the Civil War on the site of the old **(4) Manor House Hotel**. Note the confederate bias of the plaque, which

TOUR FOUR: Fun and Quirky Alexandria

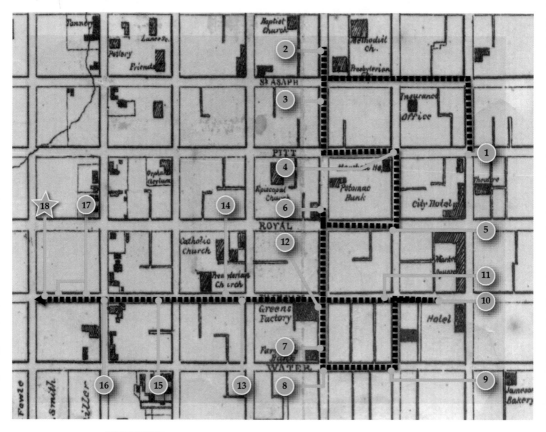

LOCATIONS

1. George Washington's Townhouse
2. 605 & 607 Prince
3. J. D. Brown House
4. Manor House Hotel
5. 112 South Royal Street
6. Spite House
7. Fairfax House
8. Athenaeum
9. Ice House
10. Carlyle House
11. Stabler-Leadbeater Apothecary Museum
12. Green's Furniture Factory
13. Friedson's Grocery Store building
14. Old Presbyterian Meeting House
15. flounder house
16. Wilkes Street Tunnel
17. Victorian homes at 509 and 509½
18. flounder house

describes the death of Confederate hotelier Jackson but not of Union general Ellsworth.

Continue east on King Street to Royal Street and turn right to **(5) 112 South Royal**. In 1799, this was the location of Joseph Ingle Cabinet Shop, which constructed the mahogany coffin in which George Washington was buried. The cabinetmaker charged the Washington estate $99.25 for the coffin, clearly missing the branding value of providing the coffin for free in exchange for advertising rights. Continue on Royal Street to Prince Street, and briefly turn right to the **(6) Spite House** (p. 71) at 403 Prince. This house is about 7 feet wide, and the interior walls are former exterior walls of the

The Carlyle House, as seen from the east (rear) side, before the removal of the old Mansion House Hotel, which sat between the Carlyle House and Fairfax Street, behind the house in this photo. (Library of Congress)

houses to the north and south. Built around 1800, recent property listings describe this this house is about 7 feet wide and 608 total square feet over two floors.

Turn around and travel east on Prince Street to the **(7) Fairfax House** (p. 50) at 207 Prince Street. In 1790, William Hodgson purchased the house, where he and his family lived happily for twenty-five years. Hodgson was a prominent Alexandria businessman and member of the Christ Church vestry. Before arriving in Virginia, though, Hodgson served two years in Newgate Prison, London, for referring to King George III as a "German Hogbutcher." This house is also traditionally said to be the first in Alexandria to have indoor plumbing, which drained directly onto Prince Street.

Continue down Prince Street to the **(8) Athenaeum** (p. 86) and turn left on Lee Street. Notice the **(9) Ice House** (p. 73) on the right, one of only two facilities still standing in Alexandria that supported the distribution of hundreds of thousands of tons of ice annually between 1900 and 1930.

Continue north on Lee Street, turn left on King Street and right on Fairfax to the **(10) Carlyle House** (p. 55). The prominent history of this mansion is augmented by the long-held belief that William Carlyle, in accordance with Scottish tradition, embedded a cat in one of the walls of the house when it was being built for good luck. Turn around and head south on Fairfax Street to get to the **(11)**

Stabler-Leadbeater Apothecary Museum (p. 76). The amazing history of this apothecary shop is augmented by the knowledge the items dispensed by Edward Stabler and his descendants included mercury, beetle extract, bloodletting equipment, and "dragon's blood."

Continue south on South Fairfax Street, passing **(12) Green's Furniture Factory** (p. 70), remembering to look for James Green's initials on the south end of the building, and **(13) Friedson's Grocery Store** building (p. 72). Continue south to the **(14) Old Presbyterian Meeting House** (p. 82). The grounds and the church itself, in addition to being one of the most notable religious institutions in the country, is reputed to be haunted by the souls of Revolutionary War soldiers and members of the Carlyle family.

Continue south on South Fairfax Street, passing the **(15) flounder house** (p. 60) at 412 South Fairfax Street. At the intersection with Wilkes Street look down into the **(16) Wilkes Street Tunnel** (p. 94). Continue down to the 500 block of Fairfax Street, noting the two Victorian homes at 509 and 509½ that were built in 1894 and share one lot—each house is 14 feet wide. Continue to the Victorian homes at 529-535 South Fairfax, each 11 feet wide. Across the street is another Alexandria flounder house, at 514 South Fairfax.

Bibliography

The maps and photographs credited to the Alexandria Library Special Collection are provided by the Alexandria Public Library, Special Collection, 717 Queen Street, Alexandria, VA 22314

Books

The Anglo Saxon Version, from the Historian Orosius by Alfred the Great, Together with an English Translation from the Anglo Saxon. London: W. Bowyer & F. Nichols, MDCCLXXIII (1773).

Chernow, John. *Alexander Hamilton*; Penguin Press, New York, 2004.

Cox, Ethelyn. Historic Alexandria, Street by Street. Alexandria, Virginia: Historic Alexandria Foundation, 1976.

Eliz, et al., editors. *Alexandria, a Composite History*; Hambleton Publishers, 1975. The chapter by Ruth Lincoln Kaye entitled "Streets and Alleys of Old Alexandria" was particularly insightful.

Freeman, Douglas Southall. *Lee*. New York, Touchstone. 1997.

Holly, O. L. *The Life of Benjamin Franklin*; New York George F. Cooledge & Brothers, 1848.

Madison, James; *The Writings of James Madison: Comprising His Public Papers and His Private Correspondence*. Edited by Hunt, Gaillard. G.P. Putnam's Sons, 1904.

Madison, Robert L. *Walking with Washington: Walking Tours of Alexandria, Virginia*. Baltimore, Maryland: Gateway Press, Inc., 2003. An excellent and rich source text with much to recommend it.

Moore, Gay Montague. *Seaport in Virginia – George Washington's Alexandria*. Charlottesville, Virginia: The University Press of Virginia, 1949. Available at http://www.hotfreebooks.com/book/Seaport-in-Virginia-George-Washington-s-Alexandria-Gay-Montague-Moore.html.

Randall, William Sterne. *Thomas Jefferson, a Life*; New York, Harper Perennial, 1993.

News Articles (listed in Smith, William Francis, and T. Michael Miller *A Seaport Saga, Portrait of Old Alexandria, Virginia*; Virginia Beach VA: The Donning Company,1989.

Sparks, Jared (editor), *The Autobiography of Benjamin Franklin*. London: Henry G. Bohn, York Street, Covent Garden, 1850.

Stacey, C.P. "The British Forces in North America during the Seven Years War." Chapter in *The Dictionary of Canadian Biography*. Toronto: University of Toronto Press, 1966.

News Articles (listed in chronological order)

"On Wednesday Last Thomas Jefferson, President of the United States, took the oath of office…". *Alexandria Times and District of Columbia Advertiser*, (May 6, 1801).

"George Washington Parke Custis…". *Alexandria Gazette Packet*, (February 24, 1855).

"Destructive Fire. Burning of the Market House and Public Offices". *Alexandria Gazette*, (May 19, 1871).

"New Year's 100 years ago…". *Alexandria Gazette*, (January 1,1876).

"The Cameron Street Improvements . . . ". *Alexandria Gazette Packet*, (May 13, 1878).

"The Story Behind a Street Rich in History". *Alexandria Gazette Packet*, (March 22, 1987).

"Ice House Makes Slick-Looking Office Building." Alexandria Gazette Packet (August 31, 1988).

"Fawcett-Reeder House for Sale." *Old Town Alexandria Patch*(February 3, 2012). Available at: http://oldtownalexandria.patch.com/articles/517-prince-street-alexandria-va#photo-9222605.

"Old Town History: Bank of Alexandria", *Alexandria Gazette Packet* (April 12, 2012). Available at:http://www.connectionnewspapers.com/news/2012/apr/12/old-town-history-bank-alexandria/.

Journals, Periodicals, and Other Publications

"Alexandria History Waterfront Plan: Alexandria, a Living History." City of Alexandria, Virginia: Alexandria Archeology Office. November 2010. Available at:http://alexandria.gov/uploadedFiles/planning/into/waterfront/AACWaterfrontHistoryPlan.pdf.

Bish, Jim. "Hugh West and the West Family's Momentous Role in Founding and Developing Alexandria and Fairfax and Loudon Counties, Virginia." *The Alexandria Chronicle*. Alexandria, Virginia: Alexandria Historical Society (Spring 2010). Available at: http://www.alexandriahistorical.org/images/stories/Chronicle/2010_Sp_Chronicle.pdf.

Miller, T. Michael. "A Stroll Through History, a Walking Tour of Historic South Lee (Water) Street." *The Alexandria Chronicle*. Alexandria, Virginia: Alexandria Historical Society(Fall/Winter 1994).Available at:http://www.alexandriahistorical.org/images/stories/94Winter-Fall.pdf.

Riker, Diane. "The Fitzgerald Warehouse: The Early History of an Alexandria Landmark." *The Alexandria Chronicle*. Alexandria, Virginia: Alexandria Historical Society (Summer 2007).Available at:http://www.alexandriahistorical.org/images/stories/Chronicle/2007_Su_Chronicle.pdf.

Riker, Diane. "Fitzgerald Warehouse, King and Union Street." City of Alexandria, Office of Historic Alexandria (2008). Available at: http://alexandriava.gov/uploadedfiles/historic/info/history/OHAHistoryWFFitzgerald.pdf.

Winston, Jr., Lewis E. Benjamin Hallowell: *Educational Leader of Virginia, Maryland, and Pennsylvania, 1799-1877*. Dissertation submitted to the Faculty of the Virginia Polytechnic Institute and State University(May 18, 1988). Available at:http://scholar.lib.vt.edu/theses/available/etd-42998-19743/unrestricted/Hallowell.pdf.

Yorke, Barbara. "Alfred the Great, the Most Perfect Man in History," *History Today*, Volume 49 Issue 10. Available at: http://www.historytoday.com/barbara-yorke/alfred-great-most-perfect-man-history

Working Papers

Miller, T. Michael (Research Historian of Historic Alexandria). "Derivation of Alexandria Street Names" (undated). Provided by the Office of Historic Alexandria, 220 North Washington Street, Alexandria VA, 22314.

Ryan, Kelsey (Office of Historic Alexandria /Alexandria Archeology). "Travelers Accounts of the Historic Alexandria Waterfront" (2009). From this fascinating and well-researched compilation came all the margin texts quoting early travelers' impressions of Alexandria. Available at: http://alexandriava.gov/historic/info/default.aspx?id=42130.

Web Pages

"Hannah Jackson Property." *African American Historic Sites Database*. http://www.aaheritageva.org/search/sites.php?site_id=482.

"Alexandria's Scottish Heritage." *Electric Scotland*.http://www.electricscotland.com/usa/alexandria/history.htm.

"American Legion Post 24, History." *The American Legion Post 24.* http://www.valegionpost24.org/content.php?id=2.

"Building Furniture, Building up the South." (Kolbe, Chris, and Jim Greve) *Out of the Box: Notes from the Archives @ the Library of Virginia* (October 26, 2011). http://www.virginiamemory.com/blogs/out_of_the_box/2011/10/26//building-furniture-building-up-the-south.

"Captain John Harper, 125 South Union Street." *Local Kicks:* http://www.localkicks.com/article.jsp?ID=589.

The City of Alexandria: The Alexandria Archeology Museum, Heritage Trail. http://alexandria.gov/HeritageTrail.

The City of Alexandria: Fitzgerald Warehouse, King and Union Street. http://alexandriava.gov/uploadedfiles/historic/info/history/OHAHistoryWFFitzgerald.pdf.

The City of Alexandria: The Freedmen Memorial. http://alexandriava.gov/FreedmenMemorial.

The City of Alexandria: The History of the Lyceum. http://alexandria.gov/historic/lyceum.

Colburn, Trevor. "The Lamp of Experience: Whig History and the Intellectual Origins of the American Revolution" in chapter VIII, "Thomas Jefferson and the Rights of Expatriated Men." *The Online Library of Liberty.* Indianapolis: Liberty Fund, 1998. http://oll.libertyfund.org/index.php?option=com_staticxt&staticfile=show.php%3Ftitle=674&Itemid=99999999.

"The Decline and Fall of Edward Gibbon." Apologies in a Post Christian Age *(blog by Trevor J. Major).* http://trevormajor.com/archives/883.

"Description of the engraving of Mount Vernon in the Monticello Dining Room." *Monticello Home Page.* http://www.monticello.org/site/house-and-gardens/mount-vernon-engraving#_note-1.

"First Blood." *The Smithsonian Institution: CivilWar@Smithsonian.* http://www.civilwar.si.edu/firstblood_floor_flag.html.

The Friends of Freedmen's Cemetery. http://www.freedmenscemetery.org/.

"Gadsby's Tavern (originally published 1932)." *Old and Sold: Turn of the Century Wisdom for Today.* http://www.oldandsold.com/articles11/virginia-homes-3.shtml.

"Gadsby's Tavern and Ice Well." *The Virginia Department of Historic Resources.*http://www.dhr.virginia.gov/SlideShows/GadsbysTavern/GadsbysTitleslide.html.

"History of the Apothecary Museum", The City of Alexandria Web Page, https://www.alexandriava.gov/historic/apothecary/default.aspx?id=36978

History Spotlight: First Metropolitan Area Free Methodist Churches.75th Anniversary Campmeeting, July 13, 2006. http://www.redpeninc.com/camp/history-13July06.htm.

*The Lee-Fendall House Museum and Garden.*http://leefendallhouse.org and http://leefendallhouse/family.

"The Marquis deLaFayette and Two Keys to the Bastille." *The Scottish Rite Journal (February 1998).* http://srjarchives.tripod.com/1998-02/Dunaway.htm.

"Top Twelve Buildings and Homes in Alexandria." *Jaybird's Jottings* (blog) (February 15, 2012). http://jay.typepad.com/william_jay/2012/02/top-twelve-buildings-and-homes-in-alexandria-.html.

The White House Website. http://www.whitehouse.gov/about/presidents.

Index

Acknowledgements

The genesis of this book came one day in 2011 while returning from a weekend fly-fishing trip with two friends, Gus Mutscher and Paul Colby. On the way back to Alexandria from the Laurel Highlands, we passed the historical marker pictured on page 9, prompting a conversation about General Braddock, the French and Indian War, and the street names in historic Alexandria. It was a fascinating, rambling conversation that led to all of us regretting that there was no authoritative reference about Alexandria, its street names, and more generally its earliest beginnings. In that moment, thanks to Paul and Gus, the concept for the book was born.

Thanks also go to Link Nicoll and Jesse Floyd. Shortly after the book was conceived, my family and I visited Link and Jesse at their summer home in Chester, Nova Scotia. There I found a musty 1966 version of The Dictionary of Canadian Biography. Inside that text I found C. P. Stacey's fascinating essay on Braddock's misadventure and the ensuing explosion of warfare around the world between France and Britain. The first outline of the book was motivated by that find.

Special gratitude goes to the staff at the Office of Historic Alexandria, particularly Amy Bertsch, Barbara Balentine, and Michael Miller. The Staff at the Alexandria Library Special Collection also went out of their way to be helpful, particularly George Combs.

I would like to thank Constance Denning of CDDesign, who was the creative mind behind the layout of the initial drafts, and Donavan Lyons who helped out with graphical support when a new set of eyes and hands was required.

A special call-out also goes to Kirstin Downey, noted author and former Washington Post reporter, who took my draft and said "Gee, that's really neat, you should find a publisher," and then referred me to her agent, Ross Yoon; from that point on all was good. Anna Sproul-Lattimer at Ross Yoon gets extra credit for her patience and wise guidance.

Old Town Alexandria, because it is such a fascinating place, has a rich history of books from which to draw both facts and inspiration. Invaluable to me and potentially fascinating to you, the reader, were Smith and Miller's *A Seaport Saga*, Gary Moore's *Seaport in Virginia*, and Michael Lee Pope's *The Hidden History of Alexandria, DC*. I am an occasional member of the Alexandria Historical Society, and reading Jim Bish's notes on the West family, published in their newsletter was another moment of clarity and acceleration.

The walking tours were tested by Claire Sharman with assistance from her mom, Kate.

Special thanks are due to my wife Jane and sons Andrew and Stuart, for being helpful and patient when it mattered most, which is to say, always.

Alexandria is a great town, and for that reason all of the author's proceeds from this text will be donated to the ACT for Alexandria, the Alexandria Library Special Collection, and the Historic Christ Church Foundation, which supports the maintenance of the building and grounds of this amazing space. All of these organizations could use your support as well.

About the Author

Frederick Knops has lived in Alexandria, Virginia, for 25 years with intervening periods residing in London, Amsterdam, Rome, and Buenos Aires. Nonetheless, Fred and his wife Jane and their sons Andrew and Stuart consider Alexandria their home. Fred is currently an executive at LendPro LLC, and previously was a Partner and Senior Vice President at Booz Allen Hamilton. He has been cited often in the press on topics of business, consulting, and technology, including appearing on the pages of the *Wall Street Journal, Barron's,* and the *Financial Times of London.* This is Fred's first book.

All of the author's proceeds from this book will be donated to ACT for Alexandria, the Alexandria Library Special Collections Unit, the Christ Church Foundation for the care of that precious building, and other Alexandria charities as administered by ACT.